FD-323 (3-28-60)

UNITED STATES DEPARTMENT OF JUSTICE
FEDERAL BUREAU OF INVESTIGATION

Washington 25, D. C.
June 14, 1961

In Reply, Please Refer to
File No.

Re: Porfirio Rubirosa

A confidential source, on March 16, 1961, advised as
follows:

Porfirio Rubirosa, who has served as
Dominican Ambassador to various European countries,
and currently occupies the position of Dominican
Ambassador to France, according to the source, is
an ███████████████████████████████████. On his

trips to the Dominican Republic, Rubirosa ███████████
Rubirosa and ████████ and following these conferences,
███████████████████████ Whenever Rubirosa arrives in
the Dominican Republic, he is given the "red carpet"
treatment, and in less than two minutes, is on his
way from the airport to either ███████. The source has learned
that Rubirosa performs important missions abroad, and
that his specialty is to influence people in influential
positions in foreign governments in a manner favorable
to the Trujillo Regime.

The source stated the fact that Rubirosa
██████████████████████████████ in his opinion,
conclusively proves that ██████████████████████

b7C
b7D

For ltiond _____
Indexed _____
Filed _____

SECRET 97-2078-4

Chasing Rubi

Chasing Rubi

The Truth About Porfirio Rubirosa
The Last Playboy
* * *
Based on His Memoirs
And the FBI File
* * *
Spy? Assassin?
Or Just a Gigolo?

Marty & Isabella Wall
with Robert Bruce Woodcox

Literary Press

Newport Beach, CA

Literary Press
3857 Birch St. Suite 702
Newport Beach, CA 92660

The author and publisher assume neither liability nor responsibility to any person or entity with respect to any direct or indirect loss or damage caused, or alleged to be caused, by the information contained herein, or for errors, omissions, inaccuracies, or any other inconsistency within these pages, or for unintentional slights against any people or organizations.

This work is based on a true story. However, due in some cases to difficulties in translating certain quoted materials that were originally in Spanish (as spoken in the Dominican Republic in the 1930s through the 1950s), some passages had to be paraphrased or translated to the best of our abilities, which might have changed the original intent somewhat. In addition, some minor artistic license has been taken with respect to Porfirio Rubirosa's quotations and memoirs for the sake of a better flow of ideas and emotions. The authors, in most of this content, have remained as faithful to the facts as current research allows.

Permission to reprint lyrics from "Just a Gigolo," by Irving Caesar, Julius Brammer and Leonello Casucci. © 1930 (renewed) Irving Caesar Music Corp. and Chappell & Co. Inc. All rights on behalf of Irving Caesar Music Corp. Administered by WB Music Corp. All rights reserved. Used by permission.

Photo credits: *See page 231*

ISBN No. 0-9764765-2-5
Library of Congress Catalogue No. 2005904444

First edition Printed in the United States of America

Acknowledgments

And so, here we are. We started this adventure in New York and it's taken us to places we never expected to go. We've chased Rubirosa through microfilm, FBI files, media reports and historical documents, and through the streets of Rio, Santo Domingo, Paris, Palm Springs, Newport and Los Angeles.

We've looked for Rubi in the faces of other Dominican dreamers and those who search exclusively for pleasure.

The chase has been delightful and chaotic, filled with passion and frustration. During our journey we have lost some friends and made many new ones. We've grown wiser, more diligent and compassionate. But most of all, we've grown to really appreciate our true friends. You know who you are.

We are blessed with your friendship. Thank you.

Dedication

We dedicate this book and all the good that comes from it, to our mothers and fathers.

To Shirley Wall and Dina Howard, thank you for patience, love and the ability to nurture the people and things we love. And, thanks for having us.

To Don Herberto Martinez and H.E. Wall Jr., thank you for confidence, fair play and a never ending desire to finish the job. We are able to do all that we dream because of you.

And a special acknowledgement to Don Herberto for introducing us to Porfirio Rubirosa.

Contents

Porfirio Rubirosa, circa 1953
The first international man of mystery

I'm just a gigolo and everywhere I go,
people want to know the part I'm playin'.
Paid for every dance, selling each romance;
ooh, what they're sayin'.
There will come a day,
when youth will pass away;
what will they say about me?

When the end comes, I know I'll be just a gigolo
as life goes on without me.

'Cause I'm just a gigolo
life goes on without me.
I ain't got nobody.
Nobody cares for me, nobody, nobody cares for me.
I'm so sad and lonely, sad and lonely, sad and lonely.
Won't some sweet mama come and take a chance with me,
'cause I ain't so bad.

"Just a Gigolo/ I Ain't Got Nobody"
– by Irving Caesar, Julius Brammer and Leonello
Casucci

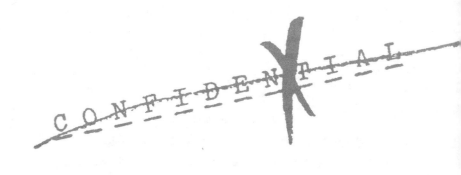

Introduction
Why Did We Chase
Rubirosa?

L ouis Prima, the big swing band leader of the '40s and '50s, made the song *Just a Gigolo* famous as Porfirio Rubirosa became known as the world's most infamous playboy—and it could have served as Rubirosa's anthem.

Prima met Rubi, as he was known to friends, through their mutual friends Frank Sinatra and Peter Lawford, who, as members of the "Rat Pack," practically lived at the Sands Hotel in Las Vegas where Prima fronted a band in the lounge. Rubirosa frequently partied there with the group in the late '50s and early '60s.

"... everywhere I go people want to know the part I am playing." There was always so much curiosity about Rubirosa by the press, the rich and powerful including our FBI and Presidents.

"When youth will pass away, what will they say about me." One thing we know is what was said about Porfirio—what we learned is a different story.

My wife and I became fascinated with Rubirosa more than 15 years ago. Isabella is from the Dominican Republic, as was Rubirosa. She first began hearing the stories about him from her father, who grew up in the same town with Rubirosa. Her father also gave her a book about Rubi's life.

From the book *Mis Memorias*, we read Rubi's own perspective on his life. Over the years, this information led to other revelations about this legendary figure that continued to captivate us both.

When we first began chasing Rubirosa ourselves, we decided to try to tell his story in a movie. It was filled with adventure, mystery, and intrigue; all the characteristics of a good film, but there were so many unanswered questions.

What was the secret to his legendary lovemaking? Did he use his diplomatic posts as a launching pad to spy for the Dominican Republic and/or other governments and individuals. In other words, was he ultimately a good or a bad guy?

Thorough observations provide valuable lessons, insights, and for us, inspiration. The way we looked at it, there is always something to be censured in every man and woman. We can approve their virtues and despise their faults (as we all have both).

No one is so good as to only deserve applause, nor as bad as to only deserve criticism. We discovered Rubi deserved both, and received an abundance of both.

Because appearances can be deceiving, there will always be those who appear to be philanthropists, who in fact are unscrupulous narcissists. It would be best, we thought, to present the good and the bad for a complete picture.

No matter what, Rubirosa was an exciting and intriguing individual who continues to stimulate many people's curiosity. As we learned more about this amazing life, we became more curious about how someone our own government claims is a spy and a murderer could end up partying on the presidential yacht with John Fitzgerald Kennedy and Frank Sinatra.

Our questions started an odyssey of inquiries, explorations, and our desire to make a movie led to multiple meetings with the usual Hollywood power brokers who make movie dreams come true.

One of our first meetings was with producer Stuart Benjamin, the Executive Producer of the movie *La Bamba* (and most recently the Ray Charles bio-pic Ray). Among other things, we learned that we were not the only Rubi enthusiasts. Writer/Director Ramón Menendez (*Stand and Deliver*) had written a script on Rubi's life.

Stuart patiently helped us through our initiation into the world of movie development. Lesson one: It takes at least ten years to become an overnight success. Stuart took our research and Ramon's script to meet with Marc Platt, then President of Tri-Star Pictures. Unbeknownst to us, biopics such as Tri-Star's *Bugsy*, were dying tragic deaths at the box office and a "Latin only" story would not be an easy sell. In short, a biopic about a Latin character was not the flavor of the month in 1991.

For the next seven years, we heard the same from many other Hollywood executives, which is when we learned lesson number two: Attach a star to your project. Letters and phone calls to Andy Garcia and Antonio Banderas were returned with a standard, "No thank you." It seemed that neither Mr. Garcia nor Mr. Banderas were interested in playing the legendary lover.

Over the next few years, rumors of various Rubirosa movies became more prevalent, including a Spanish 30–episode telenovela starring Ernest Borgnine as Trujillo, and a Mexican soap star who was rumored to play Rubirosa.

While continuing to approach Hollywood leads, we amped up our research on Rubi and assembled over 3,000 pages of articles, stories, letters, and interviews including his memoirs written in 1955. More importantly, much of Rubirosa's story has been gleaned from FBI files that we obtained through the Freedom of Information Act—documents and facts that heretofore, have never been revealed about this intriguing figure. Rather, it implies that Rubi was a rogue political figure, a spy, even an assassin, maybe tied to the Mafia, and at various times, a friend or a perceived threat to the Eisenhower and Kennedy administrations (depending on which documents you read).

Every year, after requesting the documents, the FBI wrote us to ask if we "still" wanted and needed the information. We were told repeatedly about the many other "more important" tasks they had before them and if we didn't want the documents, the agents would be free to go about that more important business. These delays made us even more curious about the playboy diplomat and caused us to once again increase our investigation—we never relented. It took a full seven years before we received all 500 pages in a plain manila wrapper, with just the return street address printed in the upper left corner—no FBI seal.

The information in these documents reflects 30-years of bureau surveillance of Rubirosa from 1935 through 1965.

Eventually, we came to a more conclusive picture of who this man really was; yet, there are still unanswered questions.

We have endeavored to portray as accurate a picture as possible of an extraordinary man who lived a remarkable life.

This is the story of an infallible, paradoxical, and noteworthy human being, possessed by an insatiable thirst for pleasure and an unbearable fear of boredom. It is the account of a man who once said, "I am, and always will be, a man enslaved by the desire for pleasure."

However, as you read, you may feel like one of the four blind men who stumbled upon an elephant.

As each of them walked around the giant animal, touching and probing in an inquisitive effort to ascertain what it was, one of the blind men—having felt the elephant's long nose—said, "Surely this beast must be like a giant snake."

The second blind man, having run his fingers over the animal's rough, corrugated hide, said, "No. This is not a snake. This animal must be like an alligator with his coarse hide."

Therefore, each of the two blind men, having touched a separate portion of the animal, went away with a different understanding or picture. So it was with us—as it is with many journalists, writers, wives, girlfriends, celebrities, and politicians—who were either intimate with Rubi, or at least acquainted with him.

Rubirosa's story is a tapestry of great theater and story-telling, complete with espionage, intrigue, fantastic wealth and above all, love. It is a story that until now has only been told in scattered bits and pieces through the various world-wide media—and then, not even in its entirety. Now, the complete story is being told.

Among all the questions answered and left unanswered, one thing is certain: We discovered Rubi's lovemaking secrets—techniques that, at one time, earned him the title of the most sensual man in the world, and the greatest playboy of the 20th century.

Rubi's father, Don Pedro Maria Rubirosa.
Adultery was a death-penalty offense, but that
didn't stop him...

Considering the caliber and sheer quantity of women that Rubi romanced and slept with, he was not considered at that time to be a particularly good-looking man. He was strong and had an athletic physique, but wasn't tall, only five feet, nine inches, which did not come close to the *minimum* six feet de facto requirement of great European lovers.

Though his parents were Hispanic, his features more closely resembled the mulatto background in his family. He had dark skin, a broad nose, and naturally curly hair, which he wore slicked straight back.

Despite not having chiseled, leading-man good looks, Rubi nevertheless provoked constant curiosity and adoration in women, particularly the wealthy and celebrated.

While we lived on a small island in the Virgin Islands, I attended a school that gave out prizes. Mine was a violin, which I knew nothing about. In addition, they placed me in the orchestra and simply told me to play.

I remember breaking down in tears in front of all the others. I had no idea how to play a violin. But the teacher said, "Porfirio. Just pretend. Pretend that you know how to play; that will be fine."

I thought: Is that how it is in the adult world? Does everyone just pretend? Those words, "Pretend you know how to play," and what they symbolized, would be etched in my mind forever. I asked myself: A trusted teacher's only advice was to feign knowing something?

– Porfirio Rubirosa (about age 6)

Writer Diogenes Reyna, who met him, had this to say: "The skillful man is the one who makes it. Intelligence sometimes betrays. The very intelligent man trusts and lets pass many details.

"When I saw Porfirio Rubirosa for the first time, I already had heard about him, about his lovers. He was very famous. I said to myself, 'Boy, this man is short. He is not tall and he's not handsome, but somehow he's attractive…so this is Rubirosa?

"After listening to him, I realized he was a great speaker. He had great eloquence and a convincing power. This was part of the clue for his conquests, and he was also very persistent.

"One of his many loves, Zsa Zsa Gabor, once remarked that Rubi was, 'charming…exciting…and volatile…' and added that he had exquisite taste, despite the fact that he once blackened her eye so badly, she wore a pirate-like eye patch for more than two weeks."

For years, the media struggled to define his attraction, alternating between, "He whips up a tempest, which anesthetizes women's reasoning powers," or, "He appears destined to be nothing more than a temporary catastrophe in a woman's life," finally concluding that his Latin American machismo must have been responsible for his extraordinary success.

European women, accustomed to a more respectful and chivalrous treatment by their suitors than their American counterparts, greatly enjoyed being treated by Rubirosa as goddesses and sex objects in exactly that order.

He was called "The Romeo of the Caribbean," a tough guy with impeccable manners; a smooth dancer, extremely well dressed at all times, with an intriguing sexy accent; an adaptable companion as irresistible to women as to his male friends.

He was a chameleon that reflected his lovers' desires, as

well as the diplomats, politicians, businessmen, and other male associates he came in contact with—as multifaceted as a mirrored ball twirling high above the dance floor.

In her memoirs, Zsa Zsa Gabor wrote:

"Mother and I went to the Persian Room and it was then that I met him. It was then that Rubi finally impressed me. He was dark, magnetic, as mysterious in his own way as Ataturk had been in his (*Ataturk was one of Zsa Zsa's lovers and a military hero who became the founder and leader of Turkey*), as cool and composed as Conrad Hilton (*Zsa Zsa's previous husband*), and as sophisticated and urbane as George Sanders (*Gabor's husband at the time she began her affair with Rubi*). Before we ever even touched, Rubi mesmerized me.

"He and I spent one night together at the Plaza and in the morning, I knew that I never wanted to leave him again. I was madly in love with George, but after one night with Rubi, I lost all sense of reality. He was exciting, sensual, passionate, and primitive…."

To fully understand how Porfirio Rubirosa came to be the whirlwind, playboy/diplomat, possessor of great fortunes bestowed upon him like a showering of diamonds by the world's richest women, and even perhaps an international spy, you should know something about the country he came from and how he was raised.

The Dominican Republic
Now and Then

What do Bill Clinton, Oscar De La Renta, Julio Iglesias, Mikhail Baryshnikov, and Oscar de la Hoya have in common? They either own real estate or rent homes on the Island of Hispaniola, discovered by Christopher Columbus, the home of the Caribbean paradise known as the Dominican Republic.

Today (2005), the country is being touted as "The new St. Barts" where tourism and luxury home construction are booming. Wealthy Americans are flocking there in droves because, though the Caribbean remains crystal blue as it always was, the sunsets are as stunning as ever, and the lush tropical landscape still beckons—prices are very low and those who were the first tourists are now settling into beautiful estates that are a third the price of St. Barts.

Some lucky investors were able to find properties close to the colonial zone where more than five centuries of history are preserved in about 100 square blocks that stand sentry over the harbor.

More than 300 astounding monuments still stand among the Spanish colonial buildings, preserving life as it was in the 1500s. Some are bronze with green patina that is testament to years of weathering in an environment of alternating blistering sun and tropical rains.

Others are concrete that confound the imagination: How were these created 500 years ago?

Walking these streets, one can almost smell history and tradition. It doesn't hurt that it's only a three-hour flight from New York, either.

This is a modern phenomenon. It wasn't always like this in the Dominican Republic. When Porfirio Rubirosa was born in 1909 in the small town of San Francisco de Macoris, the country was being shaken with war and revolt. Then president Ramon Caceras had killed the former dictator Ulises Hereaux and taken over the nation.

Like any young boy, Porfirio was profoundly affected by the violence and insecurity of war, and he was forever imprinted by those forces and by the two divergent personalities of his parents, as well as the surroundings of his beautiful island.

Historians refer to this time as "The Generalissimo Era" in the Dominican Republic because of the constant insurrection of guerilla leaders who simply granted themselves the rank of general, not because of their leadership qualities, but because they could. Even so, for the most part these self-anointed officers were well respected throughout that society.

One such general was Pedro Maria Rubirosa, Porfirio's father, who was known for his bravery, daring spirit, and superb horsemanship—traits that Rubi would inherit. Rubi would also inherit another of his father's traits—his love of women.

Don Pedro was a man with an impressive personality. He had an arrogant look, even in a relaxed state, with his strong cheekbones, powerful head, and thick mustache.

He wore a uniform of sorts: an ammunition belt, holster and pistola always strapped to his side, and a saber slung over the other hip. When in public, he wore a jacket, an officer's collar, and a Panama hat, dressing as was expected of a general at that time.

At all times, Don Pedro stood proudly erect, shoulders pulled back, head held high, with a stride that was defiant and proud.

Among other "brave" acts, the married Don Pedro loved to seduce women, a crime (adultery) punishable by death in his country at the time. Yet, Pedro didn't fear the system. However, he might have felt differently when his wife discovered he had seduced the country's most distinguished woman and then literally drug him out of a town square meeting, took him home, and waged a weeklong battle with her husband that she is said to have won.

"You are lucky you aren't in a prison, or worse, dead," she yelled at him. For the first time she could remember, her husband's shoulders were slumping and he was backing up, not in a stride, but in a shuffle.

"It is a terrible sin, and it is punishable by death. What will your children say when they are older and others ask them where their father is?" she ranted.

"They will say my father was an adulterer and he was executed by a firing squad. Is that to be their heritage, oh great general?"

For the first six years Porfirio spent in his homeland, the country was continually at war with the villagers of San Francisco de Macoris, often caught in a hail of bullets between feuding rebel factions.

The country was experiencing a political crisis with the two parties, the "Bolos" and the "Coulos," waging battle. Don Pedro was a prominent member of the Bolos Party. What separated the two wasn't so much ideology as it was simply power and the benefits that go with it.

Don Pedro was already a notable figure, recognized for his courage and fierceness. He was a bold and clever soldier that stood as the best fighter in his regiment.

Porfirio would inherit these traits, and the fighting and daring spirit would always smolder inside him. Later, as an adult, he recalled the hellish sounds of the incessant gunfire and explosions that seemed to be a part of daily life. To him, it was all a game, he would say.

The bloodshed and battles were imprinted on him at a very early age and even as a three-year-old observer, he appeared to view the carnage as a captivating film rather than the violent and dangerous reality that it was; he would later turn danger into a game and violence into fun.

These images, along with that of his father mounted atop a powerful chestnut thoroughbred in a crisp, starched brown uniform riding off to yet another battle—his tender mother standing by his side, her arm about his shoulders—created a paradoxical atmosphere of violence and tenderness.

In his memoirs, *Mis Memorias*, Rubi had this to say:

My mother always dressed in black clothes that covered every inch of her body with the exception of her hands and face. She was a devoutly religious woman. It seemed she prayed most of her waking hours. Often, I would find her in a dark corner of the house kneeling and praying softly.

On the other hand, I never saw my father pray. He was a giant to me, a man of almost superhuman strength with the appetite of an ogre, and the kindness of a god. He was quite good looking as well. All the women admired him.

Though it was strictly prohibited in our culture, womanizing or adultery was still practiced relatively frequently and my father was no exception. In fact, the high risk just made it that more appealing to him.

When my father came home near nightfall, he would arrive on an enormous steed and without dismounting, he would lean down, lift me up, and put me in the saddle in front of him and then we would gallop off into the fields. He never offered a ride to my older brother, Caesar, and certainly not to my sister, Anita.

My mother could always be heard off in the distance screaming, "Be careful, Pedro. He's so small." And father would always laugh.

I wished the galloping had never ended.

Though his environment was a paradox of violence and quiet beauty, Porfirio was nevertheless raised in an atmosphere that was, and still is known, as home to the "Caribbean's friendliest people."

He absorbed that quiet passion that was his people's identity—a passion that ran from women, to spicy food, to family and friends, and to the meringue and baseball.

In January of 1915, when Porfirio was six, his father was appointed to head up the Dominican Republic Diplomatic Mission in France (technically, he was exiled to keep him from running for office), and the family sailed to Europe. From that time forward, Porfirio was never the same.

The First World War was looming in Europe and as the passenger ship carrying the Rubirosas and others neared Gibraltar, it was stopped and boarded by British sailors looking for a spy.

Rubi's mother tried to drag him to the safety of their room, but he wrenched out of her grasp and ran out into the dense fog of the early evening. Shots had been fired on the bridge and he was intent on watching the drama unfold.

In his memoirs, he described the incident:

I heard three shots fired. My mother said it was the Germans and they were going to kill us all. I didn't care. I wanted to see the action. What a spectacle! Sailors in two different types of uniforms, guns held in the air, the high society ladies scurrying inside to safety, their delicate skin covered in shawls from the sea air.

We were told there was a spy on board, a man dressed as a woman. It was all quite thrilling—gunshots, sailors running across the deck banging on stateroom doors, and people shouting.

This was not a frightened boy, but a fascinated observer witnessing real danger as though it were merely a game.

Once in Paris, the family took up residence at No. 6 Avenue MacMahon. Unfortunately, the senior Rubirosa was denied accreditation from the French government. They discovered that as a general in the Dominican Republic years before, he had ordered the execution of two French citizens. Instead, the French government permitted him to act as

Consul General, more of a business position that didn't require accreditation.

The Germans had just sunk the Lusitania and were using Zeppelin balloons to rain fear down on Paris by dropping what seemed like a never-ending saturation of bombs under cover of night.

Buildings splintered like kindling, sidewalks were ripped apart, and shattered glass sprayed in every conceivable direction.

At night, Paris was as black as tar; no gas streetlights or home lights were lit to chart a target for the Zeppelins. No one went outside after dusk.

In stark contrast, during the day, when the skies were clear, Porfirio was taken with the charms and sights of a country far different than his own.

Wandering through the Arc de Triomphe—strolling down the Champs Elysees, marveling at the goatskin coats that were then fashionable, and going to Pearl White movies (heroine of the original popular silent movie serials, *Perils of Pauline*)—he found Paris intriguing and beguiling.

It was as if people were living two lives—a nightly terrifying existence of hiding, and then by daylight, a nearly normal lifestyle.

The air raid sirens went off nightly. Sometimes bombs would drop and sometimes not, but there was always that incessant blaring of horns. It got so that the sound of the sirens was nearly as imposing as the actual bombs and their subsequent damage.

For my father and mother, the sirens became a knee jerk reaction—whether the bombs fell or didn't, everyone still experienced the same anxieties and began to quiver with fear. There is something more frightening about destruction in the dark. No one ever saw a bomb flying through the air or even land, but we could always hear that signature whistling sound they made. That usually meant they were not headed at you. Sirens, followed by whistles, followed by great explosions and plumes of smoke. It was an odd refrain, like a symphony with all of the instruments out of tune.

One night during dinner, my father announced, "Starting tomorrow, when there are air raids, we will not go down into the basement."

My mother asked why.

"Because it is stupid. If a bomb falls on the house, we would be buried alive in the basement. I can think of nothing worse."

From that time on when the sirens started, my mother would go to some dark corner in the house with her rosary and begin to pray, and father would lie down on the floor and just twist at his mustache. I chose to sit near a window that wasn't boarded up and watch the fireworks displays.

Later that month a bomb did explode on our block and father decided it would be safer to move to Royan.

During the Rubirosas' first year in France, back home, another of the Dominican Republic's leaders had been overthrown and as a result, the American military took over the country. The Americans were training Dominican soldiers and a new face came upon the scene: Rafael Leonidas Trujillo.

The U.S. military arrived in 1916 on the tail of an invasion of Haiti. They had introduced baseball, but failed to win the hearts and minds of the people, and eventually—eight years later—they left.

With the Americans in the Dominican, Don Pedro realized he might never return home. The sovereignty of his country was being violated and he was powerless to return to his previous battlefield glory, so he immersed himself and his son in a quest to improve their collective intelligence, believing that a true politician, seriously concerned about serving his country, must never stop growing.

Don Pedro hired tutors for he and his son and began to study political science, international law, languages, and economics. He then enrolled Porfirio in the Jeanson de Sailly, an exclusive private school.

Though he'd technically been forced to go to Europe, Don Pedro relished the opportunities for his family. He wanted the two boys and his daughter to have the best possible education, and the prestige of being educated in France was unquestionable.

He sent Rubi to school in the cultivated world of La Fontaine, Victor Hugo, Balzac, and the wonders of the Eiffel Tower, the Seine River, and Versailles. To live there was a distinction for Latin Americans, but Don Pedro sent the older children, Anita and Caesar, to school in Barcelona, Spain, feeling they would do better studying in their native language, while Porfirio was still young enough to benefit from schooling in Paris.

Porfirio, preferring sports, girls, and the various adventures Paris had to offer, failed most of his classes. His father became concerned not only for his son's poor study habits, but his weak physical condition. He was often sick and was losing weight. To strengthen his son's health as well as his discipline, Don Pedro enrolled Porfirio in boxing lessons. There, the young boy heard grand stories about the champions of his era: Dempsey, Carpentier, and Gunemer. These stories and the tactics he was learning seemed to suit him well. Soon he gained weight and muscle, became quite enthusiastic for the sport, and his studies improved.

The adult men he came in contact with when he was 13 were always sharing colorful accounts of their exploits—stories about the dazzling nightclubs, the jazz, the wild dancing, the heavy drinking, and half-naked cabaret girls were recounted in detail—all of which were just too much for a wild young Dominican boy to stay away from—a training ground of sorts for his many future adult exploits.

Ah, the fun I was missing, the action. The stories the men told transported me, at least in my mind, to another place; a wonderful existence where the fun never ended. There was no war. There were no worries and tomorrow would always bring a new adventure. Every night, I would wait breathlessly for the sun to rise again, so that another adventure would unfold.

The recounts of the adults' exploits filled me with anticipation. I couldn't wait to "grow up," to be a man, to romance the beautiful women with my astounding dance skills and my capacity to hold my liquor as they did.

Visualizing the cabarets they described, I could taste it, the cloud of beer and wine and smoke; someone playing the guitar, the tremors and trills, the quavers and quips, the hips gyrating, the throbbing and thrusting of the tango and the meringue. All the while, the women gathering around me, begging to dance, their champagne glasses overflowing as they flirted, smiling and winking at me.

I ached to be a part of it all.

Flashing forward a few decades, we get a glimpse of those future exploits from an article that appeared in *The New York Times Magazine* in the spring of 2001, written about him when he was in his forties.

"Porfirio Rubirosa was offered a post by Trujillo as the Ambassador to France, which turned out to be Rubi's launch pad into the Rivieran society. Handsome, opportunistic, and astonishingly 'sportif,' Rubi soon became a permanent fixture on the Cote D'Azure, or French Riviera, displaying to great effect his remarkable gambling skills at the casinos in Monte

Carlo and racing up and down the French Riviera in his 1955 Ferrari 500 Mondial Spyder at a reputed 120 miles per hour.

"By the time his ambassadorship fizzled, he had found other ways to maintain his glamorous lifestyle; these nearly always involved beautiful women.

"Rubirosa was a playboy's playboy, a keen race driver, a talented skier, pilot, and an even more talented polo player possessed of a certain indefinable charm that the ladies—Marilyn Monroe, Angie Dickenson, Eva Peron, and many others—clearly found irresistible."

✗

In the mid-1920s, though he was only 13, Porfirio was already giving his parents and French society a glimpse of the future El Rubirosa.

In those days, American jazz and the Argentine tango were all the rage in Montmarte clubs like Florence's, Le Zelli's, El Garron, and Le Perroquet—exclusive clubs frequented by the wealthy who could spend a small fortune in a single evening without a second thought.

Porfirio convinced his friends to join him at one of these hotspots.

Though he experienced an odd combination of emotions—fear, joy, and hesitation—that did not prevent him from enjoying himself. In a frenzy, he danced the Charleston and sang aloud with the jazz and blues singers.

During the slow, romantic tunes, he stole the opportunity to dance passionately cheek-to-cheek with beautiful women twice his age, drank until dawn, and eventually suffered the wrath of his parents who had been up all night frantically visiting hospitals, police, and friends' homes.

It is said that during the course of development, the changes undergone by a child entering adolescence bring with them a certain *uncertainty* about their parents. The teen years were marked by a propensity for rebelliousness and a search for new experiences, which are forbidden to them. It is also the time that the body is racing ahead of good judgment.

Even having suffered his father's wrath and reprimand, Porfirio had now been exposed to a world of parties and pleasures that would be viewed later as the decisive push, which launched his popularity in Europe as well as in the United States.

It was in Paris that I became a man. I'd missed my opportunity at home. It is a Dominican custom that fathers take their sons, when they are 12, to a prostitute. And the visit isn't just for half an hour—it lasts for days, during which time you are given the "other" part of your education.

I did not return home until I was 19, after the rights of manhood.

Less than a year after arriving in France, Don Pedro received an unexpected appointment for a diplomatic mission in England. He and Porfirio's mother, Ana, were relieved, feeling it presented the perfect opportunity for them to whisk Porfirio away from the "evil" temptations of Paris. Upon arriving, Don Pedro enrolled Porfirio in a boarding school in Calais, close to London.

Rather than study, Porfirio preferred his boxing lessons and then subsequent afternoon visits to a bar he had discovered on his way to school.

People we spoke to, who still live in the Dominican Republic, all said nearly the same thing about Porfirio—he never did like being a boy. He always wanted to be a "grownup." So, from his earliest years he tried to act the part—hanging around adults, smoking, chasing girls or women.

Isabella's father, Don Heberto Martinez, told a story about Rubi approaching him for cigarettes one day, or money to buy them. Even as a young boy, Rubi wanted to be something he was not. In this case, a boy smoking looked more like a man. It was also a sign of his persistence. Don Heberto said that when he turned Rubi down, he continued down the street asking everyone he saw for a cigarette until he got one.

Even at a young age, Rubirosa's desire to deceive to get what he wanted was showing, or perhaps, as he speculated in his memoirs, "Pretend you know how to play," was a more appropriate observation.

I had no great scholastic aptitude or a desire to work. Books did not interest me either and my teachers considered me to have no dedication. However, when I started to take boxing lessons from a professor M. Petiot, I was a different student altogether.

Petiot was an extraordinary character that smoked a pipe while giving us lessons, jabbing the air with his fists, to show us specific offensive moves; the smoke from the pipe that never left his lips, swirled around his head as he described what he was doing.

After our workouts, he would entertain us with tales of famous boxers and other colorful characters.

The same was true at school where I would gather around the older students and listen to their fascinating stories on the playground. They talked of cabarets and the craziness of jazz and about all the near-naked women.

The younger boys like myself were forced to wear shorts (a sort of uniform), which we all hated, me in particular because it meant I wasn't to associate with the girls or go into any of the cabarets. Only the older boys could wear long pants, and how I longed for long pants!

However, in 1925, I managed to steal a pair. It was my first time and I was in Montmarte with friends, one of whom was a Chilean boy named Pancho, whose family had also moved to Paris. Another boy was the son of the Maharaja of Kapurthala. Jit was his name. I was the oldest in the group.

Before we left the house, to give us courage, I raided my father's alcohol supply. Those who do not know the Paris of the twenties don't know what a "boite de nuit" (boy-du-nwee) is. Let me explain. Every night people would get together to listen to American Jazz, the orchestras, and dance the Argentinean Tango.

It was a cosmopolitan world. The adults and at least one boy drank cocktails at the Ritz, ate dinner at Maxim's, then drank champagne someplace else—all crazy games that make boys and men spend money and grow lazy.

The "boites" were clubs for the wealthy and spoiled. The basic clientele was always the same. In 1925, you had to spend a lot to be able to participate in these parties. The boites were exclusively for the rich who dedicated themselves only to pleasure. Their attitudes about life had a profound effect on me.

Writing my memoirs now, years later (1955), I still remember my first night at a boite. I can see it as vividly as if it were yesterday. I can even remember the bouncer's face as my friends, Jit, Pancho, and I entered the door in our long pants. The club was a swirl of colored lights and the band was playing the Charleston. Couples were dancing and women kicked up their high heels wearing thin skirts that barely covered their rear ends.

Everyone was laughing and the trumpets were blaring. The smell of perfume, cigarette smoke, and aftershave filled the air. I chose a beautiful woman that was seated with her date to dance with me. I will never forget her moist wet lips that parted to reveal brilliant white teeth and her enormous brown eyes. She ran her fingers through my hair as we danced close and pressed our cheeks together.

Before I knew it, it was daylight, 7 a.m. I had forgotten

that I was still a child dependant upon my parents. Suddenly, I began to worry. My mother and father had probably been up all night crying, praying, and looking for me. My father would be furious and my mother would be inconsolable.

When I returned home, I hesitated before ringing the bell. When I could finally raise my hand to push the button, the maid answered. She said, "The Mister and Missus are in the living room."

They already got up? I asked.

"No. They never went to bed."

The living room door opened and there stood my father, dark bags under his furrowed eyes. I braced for the worst, but my father just reached out to me. I ran to him. Thus the child who is born from the mother's pain, does not turn into a man until he has caused pain and suffering to his parents.

I did not believe I was a bad person, but I did feel responsible for their anguish.

To appease my guilt, I made two resolutions: to work harder and to stay focused on my studies.

I was so confused. I only wanted one thing: to start over. Yet, one of the characteristics of my nature was that I was a man made for pleasure. Would my father realize that I couldn't help myself?

✗

Because of his carousing, it wasn't long before Rubi was expelled from school and sent back to Paris by his father to study under a tutor, which, of course, suited Porfirio perfectly, now that he was free from his parents and Britain, and back in his favorite playground.

In 1928, 13 years after they arrived in Europe, the Rubirosas returned to Santo Domingo. Don Pedro's health was failing, the Americans were gone, and once again, rebellion dominated the political landscape at home.

A new name was devising a plot to overthrow the government of Horacio Velasquez. As with the other generals, the rebel, Rafael Trujillo, had pinned a star on his own lapel.

Porfirio was left alone in Paris to finish his studies. It wasn't surprising that his name didn't appear among the list of promoted students—at the age of 19, he managed to fail to graduate a third time.

Upon being notified of his son's grades, Don Pedro wrote and ordered him to return to Santo Domingo immediately. Porfirio was sorely disappointed; he had barely begun to savor his freedom and the charms of Paris.

As much as I loved Paris, I had to admit that going home again made me happy. I left as a little boy, but the memories were still vivid because my parents kept them alive with all their extraordinary stories.

I began dreaming of my native forests, the horses galloping on the beaches bordered by coconut palms, the warmth, the music, the colonial Spanish architecture, and all the marvelous exoticism—things that Europe could never replace.

For some reason, I always remembered the mist-covered summit of Pico Duarte rising more than 10,000 feet above the forests into the clouds, and I distinctly remember the times my father took me to the waterfalls that cascade down the mountains, where he would let me swim and explore the caves under the falls. It was paradise.

Aboard the Carimare, I thought of the reprimands that I would have to withstand from my father, but that did not dull my impatience. The last night on the ship I stood on deck so I could watch the white coral rise on the coast of the island.

Instead of disembarking in Santo Domingo, we pulled into port at the northern end of the island nearly 200 kilometers from the capital and home. What a journey. I had to cross all the provinces in a small French Citroen car. The trek across all those dirt roads (few were paved then) was an adventure in itself. The car shook and rattled the entire way, kicking up great plumes of yellow dust.

Each time we passed a village, groups of children would run out to wave; a passing car was a rare event. Though it was close to harrowing in places, the 10-hour journey was nothing short of enchanting.

As I opened the front door, I steeled myself for the reception, but my father was so happy to see me that he forgot to be severe.

"I was wrong, so wrong, to leave you alone in Paris," he said as he embraced me.

Relaxing his arms, he stood back to take a good look at me. I was amazed, though, at how much he'd aged. His cheeks were now sunken and gray. Dark circles fell like shadows under his eyes and his hair had thinned terribly. He was getting old. Compared to the vibrant man I'd known, he looked sad and tired....

...I had returned from Paris, the liberated son from the liberated city, parading all the prestige that conferred. It seemed everyone was envious of my emancipated behavior.

In 1928, the culture in Santo Domingo, compared to that of Paris, was like stepping back in time—way back. You couldn't just ask a girl out to the movies and be alone with her. If a young man liked a girl, he had to first ask her parents' permission in an eloquent manner. A simple yes or no was out of the question; it was more like the third degree.

In addition, if you did receive permission, you would still be chaperoned by a grandmother or an aunt. These customs now seemed ridiculous and archaic to me, having worn long pants, danced to a fevered sweat, and having been seduced by a woman twice my age.

A typical day consisted of hanging out with friends. We would go to the beach or to Colon Park, or to El Conde Street. Mostly, we would mill about waiting for the schoolgirls to come by so that we could piropos (flirt with and flatter them).

"You're marvelous," I would say to one. "You're divine," I would say to the next. "I'm going to stand under your window tonight and serenade you," I would say to another.

By this age, I'd already learned to play the piano, guitar, and even the ukulele, and my friends said I had a penchant for hypnosis. Sometimes, I would use those talents and powers to try to subdue the young girls. As a particularly pretty one passed, I would lightly strum a sensual tune on the guitar and say, "Come on. Let me hypnotize you, my dear."

To be sure, this did not often work. There were two unspoken rules then. First, you were never to touch the girls and second, they never responded, though many giggled and blushed, but would always keep their eyes fixed forward.

One day, as we were going through this ritual, a cute young girl turned and smiled back at me. I approached her and accidentally brushed her arm unintentionally.   She jumped back as if I had burned her. Coincidentally, we were standing in front of the Café 22-22, and she called out to her uncle who happened to be seated there.

He came running out in a rage and started insulting my group and then he reared back, balled up a fist, and took a swing at me. I was thankful at that moment for all my boxing lessons. Instinctively, I ducked and came back with a round house, a miracle punch to his chin that sent him to the sidewalk. As he laid there dazed, his friends came out and helped him back inside and we returned to our "post."

However, that wasn't the end of it. About a half hour later, the man came back out, his cheek as red as a pomegranate. He was huffing and puffing as he came close. I put my fists up, preparing to continue the fight, and he said, "Sir, we will now fix this."

If you say so, I replied as I raised my arms.

"No, not that way. We will have a serious duel. Are you armed?" he asked.

No, I replied emphatically.

He then opened his jacket where, shoved in his belt, was an enormous butcher knife.

"Well, I am," he said. "Come with me," he continued. "We're going to find you a big knife too."

I had never fought with a knife, but it was impossible to back down at that point.

Wait for me, I bravely told my friends. This will only take a minute. In reality, I was petrified.

I followed behind the man until he came to a store, but there were no knives for sale. Then we went to another and another. No store had any large knives. Suddenly, the man stopped and turned to me, "Do you have a revolver?" he asked.

No, of course not.

"Doesn't matter. I have a friend nearby who owns one. Let's go see who's lucky, who shoots first. Is that okay?"

The more I thought about it, the more ridiculous the whole incident seemed. The conversation was turning almost polite.

"By the way, who are you?" he asked.

I'm general Rubirosa's son.

"General Rubirosa?" He was startled.

"In that case, I cannot duel with you. I served in the army under your father. He is a good man."

Even as a young man, Porfirio was quickly realizing the benefits of a name and a reputation.

Those days would have been enchanting if it had not been for my father's decline. I would awaken early to the marvelous tropical mornings. It was heaven in the Dominican. I loved the food, the "Criollo" cuisine: rice, beans, fish, and meats all stewed together in spicy sauces and, of course, I loved all the pretty girls in their pastel dresses.

During the time I'd been gone, though, a new dance had been invented, one I'd never seen. It was called the meringue, a hybrid of African and Latin rhythms. It was played by full bands in the cities and by three-piece groups in the countryside. Dancers moved only from their hips down, shuffling to an up-tempo 2/4 beat. I became very good at it.

In the evenings, after dancing, I would stroll along the dark alleys where the small windows were protected with delicate lace curtains. I would serenade the ladies in the windows above, and when the evenings were over, I would return home exalted by having seen the fluttering of a curtain by a trembling hand.

Unfortunately, my father was becoming more ill by the day. I was so saddened to see this strong, virile man turning into a frail shell. He had worked his body to the limit.

The politics he'd been so much a part of all his life had now become a saddle of stress. The so-called democracy was a disaster. Military dictatorship was not desirable and because of these conditions, he separated from Velasquez and the Progressive party and instead, united himself with his former "telegrapher" commander of the Dominican Armed Forces, Rafael Trujillo.

As my father became grave, I sat at his bedside for days. He told me about his youth and all his adventures, his mistakes in getting involved with the chaos and the civil war, and the anguish that he experienced for the good of his country.

I, too, loved my beautiful country and hoped that someday I might serve her nearly as well.

✗

Don Pedro's health had seriously declined and he retired to his village of San Francisco de Macoris where he died in 1930. Porfirio was 21. That same year General of the Army, Rafael Trujillo took over power and would remain president for the next 30 years—most of Porfirio's adult life.

Oddly enough, though school had never been his strong suit, with the help of private tutors, after his father's death, Porfirio became a professor of French at Liceo de San Fancisco de Marois and among his pupils was the prominent Dominican Republic writer and diplomat, Alfredo Fernandez Simo.

At the same time, Porfirio's social popularity was growing. In a neighboring city, San Lazar, he set up a boxing square where the young, local athletes could have matches. He charged two cents per person to enter the ring.

When two men would fight and a crowd would grow around the makeshift ring, Porfirio would take the opportunity to serenade the girls with his ukulele (he had become a master). With a large smile and a few stanzas, he would captivate the women and provide a vivid contrast for the violence only yards away.

I would serenade the beautiful girls with a divertimento not only to flirt with them, but also to bring attention to the fights. Sometimes, as one boy was pulverizing another, I would pick up the tempo and strum vigorously as if providing background sounds for the matches.

Because of these "shows," I could sense that I was quickly becoming very popular, both with the girls and the athletes.

Generalissimo Rafael Trujillo
Big man on a small island

I n the autumn of 1932, Porfirio Rubirosa met "El Generalissimo" for the first time. By this time, Porfirio had carved out a reputation in Santo Domingo as a playboy and Trujillo was looking for young, popular, upper-class youths to help him form a conciliatory bond between his government and the upper classes.

Porfirio seemed to be a leader among the young elite, if only from a social standpoint, and since Trujillo was replacing the old guard and aides with a new Military Corps composed of just such young men, Porfirio was an obvious fit.

Rubi was summoned to the palace, and in his typical demeanor, he did not seem to be anymore impressed with the general than any other citizen. However, the general's offer was clearly powerful and persuasive. It didn't take Porfirio long to see the advantages of becoming an officer in the general's military regime, though he knew little about the man.

When the Americans pulled out of the Dominican in 1924, they left Trujillo in charge of the Dominican National Guard.

In 1930, he ran for president against Horacio Velasquez and fraudulently claimed 95-percent of the vote.

Porfirio would soon be given a unique opportunity to serve the new president with assignments that would eventually cover three decades.

I met Trujillo in the fall of 1932. I only knew him through my father and the few things he told me just before he died. They all called him, "The Tiger." I was told this tiger was more astute than any fox. Everything he planned in his life worked out, including his election, which he won in a landslide by cheating.

Those in high society ridiculed him because of his low social origins, and he was well aware of that. In fact, he went to great lengths to meet me, and others like me. He portrayed himself as a descendant of a Spanish soldier and a French Marquis, which of course, he wasn't.

He loved to tell the story that his descendants were conquistadors that came to the Americas in capes, swords at their sides, and crosses on their chests.

These stories only made the Dominican aristocracy laugh. Trujillo was an unpolished stone. His paternal grandfather had been an officer in the Havana police department. His father was a bastard son who had married a young woman of modest means from San Cristobal. They had seven children; Rafael Leonidas was the second.

He quit school at 13 and went to work as a telegrapher. Two years later, he was married to Aminta Ledesma who bore him a daughter, Flor de Oro. Quite by accident, he went from tele-grapher to the police force in 1918 and then was sent to the eastern province to deal with the resistance.

I met him at a party at the Country Club. He seemed intent on singling me out and that very evening, he invited me to join the military as an officer.

I was surprised and a bit relieved as it was the only deal I had going at the time. My friends and I celebrated all night at Trujillo's behest and with his expensive Charles I Champagne.

At ten in the morning the next day, with a demonic headache and puffy eyes, I arrived at Trujillo's office as requested. I knew that he had partied all night as well and it was amazing to me how well he stood up. Here he was a 40-year-old man who could drink and dance and smoke cigars all night and still be at his desk early in the morning, clean shaven, in his crisp uniform, and in good humor.

"Well, Rubirosa, did you have a good time last night?" He asked with a huge smile on his face.

Very nice, thank you.

"Very well. Now, on to important matters," he said.

At that point, he called out to an officer, "I have named Mr. Rubirosa a lieutenant and I want to see him in uniform as soon as possible. Take him to my personal tailor, and then to the shoemaker and the gunsmith's. He will start right away, this evening, at the Military Training center. You are personally responsible for all of these things," he told the officer.

I was quite vain in those days, so much so that I almost believed he chose me for my own merits. Deep down, though, I knew better.

It was in the military school where I learned how to play polo. I loved it the second I climbed on to the gorgeous chestnut quarter horse assigned to me. In 1933, I led our team to victory over the Nicaraguans, a mean feat considering they were the best in the world at the time.

That victory catapulted me to prominence, not only in the military but in general in the country. From that point on, I always felt the president was using me as a trophy of sorts. He would always have me around to charm the wives of visiting diplomats and dignitaries with my polo stories and other wild tales I just made up.

Trujillo obviously took a liking to the young man, and appointed him Aide-de-Camp, a position usually held by a major, and soon they appeared everywhere as two good friends. This aroused the jealousy of other officers, which the president chose to ignore.

One night, in his capacity as Aide-de-Camp, Porfirio

attended a formal state dinner and was supposed to have been in a full dress, crisp white linen uniform, standing ceremoniously behind the president at the head table.

All the military men in attendance were in formal dress uniforms. The civilian males were tidy, all in black tie tuxedos, and the women were resplendent in long evening gowns.

Each table was set with pure white bone china and crystal, a large beautiful bouquet occupying the center.

Rubirosa showed up in a simple khaki day outfit, with an air and a look of blithe indifference. As he entered, the room became hushed. First, the clanging of silverware stopped, then the chatter subsided and, finally, even the whispers disappeared. All eyes were on the brash young lieutenant.

Everyone stared in horror, wondering what Trujillo's reaction would be. Eyes darted first from Porfirio to Trujillo and then back to Porfirio. The president was known as a meticulous man in matters relating to etiquette. Surely, he would never tolerate the breaking of protocol.

At first glance, Trujillo did a double take, then turned to his left and whispered into the ear of an aide. After the attendees sat in silence for a full minute, the president finally cleared his throat and then waved to the orchestra leader without saying a word. Once the music had started, the room was again filled with chatter, only now it was conjecture. Would Porfirio be admonished in private, or worse?

Apparently, Porfirio, as arrogant as he was, was not amused at the thought of standing like a footman in front of the aristocrats of Santo Domingo. Perhaps his excuse to the president saved him, telling him privately that he had only that morning been told he would be on duty and his dress uniform was still in the laundry, which was a lie.

Already, the two were showing signs of using each other for their own purposes, a sort of mutual aid society of two that would continue for decades.

In addition to appearing in the equivalent of a sports coat,

Porfirio did not stand ceremoniously or otherwise behind the president. Instead, he chose to survey the crowd for attractive women. Within minutes, he found one beautiful young woman making eye contact with him and when the music started, he could not contain his excitement any longer. He approached the stunning black-haired beauty, bowed, and with a big grin on his face asked if she would join him at a small table near the president's.

The woman was Flor de Oro, the first-born daughter of Trujillo, though he didn't know that. She was 17 and Porfirio was 23.

Flor Trujillo
Daddy's girl

As I learned more about Flor's father, I found out that Trujillo's political victory was due in part to his army and his appeal to the middle and low socioeconomic classes in the country, who made up the bulk of the population.

Because he wanted the blessings of the aristocracy as well, he chose young men like me to serve him. I just came along at the right time and with my father's prestige and my Parisian "education," I was a good choice—I had a lot of influence with other youths of my generation and lineage.

Trujillo's protection gave me great leeway, allowed me to see the good side of military life, and to be active in sports, which I loved, especially riding horses.

It was a symbiotic relationship, although I didn't trust the man much, nor did I particularly like him.

My new life was much more physical than before and far more disciplined, which I hated. Most of the day was spent in workouts, weapons training, target practice, horseback riding, and various sports like soccer. I also learned how to fly a plane and would later obtain my twin-engine license.

Another difficult facet of military life was the horrendously early wakeup call. We were up at 5:00 a.m. every day; usually the sun wasn't even up, though when I wasn't on duty, I could stay in the city and sleep later and on a soft bed instead of cots in the tents we were sequestered in at camp.

I had many good friends in the Army and we spent as much time in the local bars as we did with sports and training. We were a rowdy bunch. In addition, of course, we loved that the women loved our uniforms. However, you must remember that Santo Domingo in those days was more like the 18th century than the 20th. For example, if on your wedding night you found out that your bride was not a virgin, it was perfectly all right to return her to her parents, as if she were no more than tarnished chattel.

Because of the social restrictions, romancing a woman was not easy. It required the complicity of maids and chauffeurs, having a secluded place to meet and above all, a young lady who was as brave and daring as she was beautiful and would not change her mind at the last minute.

I will never forget the raving beauty that I spirited away one evening. My love, you are the light of my life, I said, though I'd only known her for a few days. My desire for you is as vast as the distance from our shores to the moon. Share with me what is in your heart, so that we may draw close in the duet of love.

She nearly swooned with the syncopation and beauty of my words, and I could sense she was damp with anticipation as we planned our rendezvous.

Her father was a colonel in the army, a particularly scur-rilous man, and I knew we would need the help of his chauffeur, though I didn't particularly trust him but had no other choice or ally.

The chauffeur was an unhappy man with heavy eyelids, who walked, or rather shuffled, without ever lifting his feet from the pavement. However, he did arrive as planned, the raven-haired beauty in tow.

Seduction itself is a sweet story, though this particular evening turned out to be far more than merely seductive. Enticing is a mutual experiment in which I seemed to instinc-tively understand that a man must conspire with a woman, to give her an opening to do what she really wants to do anyway.

A woman and her principles are always at odds, so it was important not to remind my raven that she was acting against her own precepts. Unfortunately, the conspiratorial nature of our rendezvous did tend to keep this foremost in her mind, so my work was cut out for me.

Being a gentleman, I won't trace our path that evening but to say that the chauffeur's greed and the subsequent guilt-rid-den raven-haired island girl nearly cost me my freedom, at the very least, and my hide at worst.

The fat-lipped chauffeur demanded twice my original bribe and the girl threatened to confess her sins not only in church, but also to her surly father, who would have had me drawn and quartered had I not calmed the young lady, not with logic, but with the promise of further romance.

Now, many years later, I remember those days as among the happiest times, filled with camaraderie, sports, and adventures.

Shortly after I was named Aide-de-Camp and more pre-cisely the morning after I'd met Flor, Trujillo called me into his office to introduce me more formally to his daughter. I did not know it, but she had been living in Paris for several years and so we had much to discuss.

That summer the president decided to visit his vacation home in San Jose de las Matas. As Aide-de-Camp, I was invited along with several other guests and Flor, of course.

During the day, she spent a great deal of time walking in the gardens, but I kept my distance. One night shortly after our arrival, we managed to meet and our conversation became quite animated. I enjoyed her; she was stunning— with hair as black as a starless night—and smart. We talked for quite some time.

About an hour into our dialogue, I heard a window slam nearby; it was the president's suite. I thought nothing of it and we continued late into the night laughing and talking.

The next morning close to noon, thunder struck. Apparently, Flor's mother had been listening intently to us. By lunchtime, I received an order from Colonel Piro Estrella relayed from the president. It simply said, "Lieutenant Porfirio Rubirosa is confined to the fortress of San Francisco de Macoris."

I was stunned and outraged. This disgrace would surely have me thrown out of the military. My career was over for simply talking to the president's daughter?

That afternoon I was deeply depressed, which is quite unlike me. As I packed, all I could think about was that the party was over; a hard life awaited me. I might actually have to go to work. At that moment, I saw a young boy running across the courtyard. He came bounding up to my window and asked if I was alone. When I replied yes, he handed me a letter from Flor.

"Dear Porfirio: I was informed that you have to leave. I am so sorry. I hope to see you soon. I am very upset about all this and sad. I do hope we can see each other again soon. Flor"

The next day I arrived at the fortress. The look on the captain's face said it all and confirmed my nightmare. His eyebrows were pulled down in a sort of half-angry, half-disgusted look. To be sure, he was cautious of his career, knowing he had just received someone who had fallen from grace.

As it turned out in the ensuing days, my depression left me quickly as I'm not one to worry for too long about anything. I met some other lieutenants, shared our respective "criminal" causes for incarceration, had a few drinks, and even saw a few cute faces. Life in exile, it seemed, was not that bad after all.

After I'd been in the fortress for several weeks, I got a phone call. It was Flor. Her voice was like the sweetest music I'd ever heard.

"Porfirio, next week there is going to be a ball and I would like to see you," she said.

I couldn't believe she was inviting me to her home. What would her father say or do?

What time is the party? I asked.

"At five. Please come. I beg you."

Not knowing exactly what to say, I blurted out: I'll do my best. Then the phone went dead.

Though I was technically in exile, I wasn't in prison. I needed an excuse to go to Santiago, which was about 80 kilometers from the fortress. Then I remembered there was a doctor, a throat specialist there that I'd once visited, a Dr. Grullo. I pretended to have a bad sore throat, even faked a raspy low voice when I asked the captain for authorization to see the doctor.

"Write out a request and I'll send it to the department chief," he said. On the following Saturday, I had my official papers with the proper seals to go to Santiago. The ball was being held in the local Youth Club, a large wooden building. There was a magnificent orchestra, hundreds of flowered garlands and other decorations, and many of the society people. It was a classic ball held in honor of the president's daughter.

Scanning the crowd, I spotted Flor in the middle of a group of friends. We looked at each other and she was smiling as if she were in a dream. Just then, the music started and I approached her and held out my hand. She put hers gently in mine and we spent the rest of the night dancing.

Today, this would not be important, but in that time and in that society, dancing with one woman for more than three dances was considered rude and against all rules of decorum, unless it was your betrothed. I was inadvertently creating yet another scandal.

I think it was after the fourth or fifth dance, when I fell madly in love. It hit me like a powerful drug. Suddenly my legs were weak; my head, light. We drank champagne all night and spoke to each other in French, which was yet another "shocking" thing to do.

At eight o'clock, the ball was over. Flor and I, accompanied by her chaperone, strolled through the park. I had forgotten all about her father and was gliding on air. However, he hadn't forgotten me and had been alerted during the evening that I was at the ball dancing with his daughter.

We parted at nearly ten o'clock, both deeply in love and sure that all the taboos and the anger of her father would just disappear.

Knowing, even at that young age, what I knew in my every fiber about women, I knew that Flor, like every woman who is in love—whether she truly knows the man yet or not—wants to say, "Him, over there. He is the one. Unwrap him and send him to me posthaste so that he can love me!"

Since Flor could not say this, what with being the president's daughter and a staunch Catholic, I had to speak for her. I had to help the words tumble from her lips. I told her as she left: Flor, I would but hold your hand and find divine release and then you can shoot me and I will die a happy man.

When Flor returned home, she was ordered into her father's study but she refused and locked herself in her room. In minutes, he was pounding furiously on her door, but Flor didn't budge. She was the only person in the Dominican

Republic that could stand up to the Generalissimo. When he couldn't gain entrance to his daughter's room, he turned his anger to me. Once he discovered how I'd gotten out of the fortress, he ordered that I be promptly kicked out of the army.

Within the hour, my pistola was gone, my uniform confiscated, and I was literally shown the front gate. I was a civilian again. I went to stay with my grandfather to sort through the entire mess. My first thought was to return to Paris, but I didn't want to lose Flor. I loved her dearly.

The next day Lieutenant Castillo, a friend, visited me. Essentially, he told me that the whole thing was quite serious, that I should go hide. Though he didn't come right out and say it, I knew he meant that I might be shot. That is when my grandfather sent me to a secluded cacao plantation: no phone, no mail.

I sat and stewed for weeks with nothing to do. Then one day a messenger arrived and told me to go to a specific public phone at the entrance to a park. I was to arrive at 9:00 p.m. and wait for a call. It was quite dark, only a few weak flickering lights spread around the various footpaths. I found the phone and waited. Within a minute, it rang. It was Flor.

"My love, don't give up," were the first words from her lips. "Everything will work out, you'll see. I have not left my room but I have sent word to my father that I want to marry you."

She'd beaten him. She got what she wanted—always, and I was what she wanted.

I love you, I said. I love you.

I took the opportunity to call my mother from that phone and to beg her to go to see Trujillo. She must have been quite convincing because within days, I was granted permission to see Flor for just a few hours a day. He had even begrudgingly given his permission for us to marry. During those few hours we were allowed each day, we spent the time planning our wedding.

Despite her father being adamant they not marry, Flor had won the war, and the two were eventually wed in December of 1932. First, she appealed to her father's vanity by telling him that if he kept objecting to her marriage, she should not be a worthy daughter for him. Trujillo took this as a compliment, but still did not relent until finally, frustrated and angry, Flor threatened to kill herself if she were not allowed to marry the man she loved, so her father relented.

The wedding ceremony was held in the Capital Cathedral on the 3rd of December. Archbishop Nouel officiated and most of it was in Latin, so I didn't understand it all even though I spoke several languages. When Flor nodded to me, it was my signal to say, I will, or I do.

The Cathedral was an imposing building with soaring gothic ceilings and hundreds of stained glass windows through which the bright midday sun streaked—all very high Catholic drama. It was quite intimidating, particularly when the grand pipe organ began to bellow out a wedding hymn. I wore a black tuxedo, Flor wore her mother's elaborate wedding gown, complete with a veil, and a train that stretched halfway back to the entrance.

The following day, as was the custom, we celebrated with a civil ceremony in a small village, which was more to my taste—the champagne flowed well into the night and Trujillo did not smile nor utter a word. On the 5th of December, I was officially the son-in-law of Generalissimo Rafael Leonidas Trujillo Molina, Honorable President of the Republic and Benefactor of the Country.

My father-in-law was a sort of Jekyll and Hyde. He brought order, organization, and peace to our country, but his main objective was power. I have to admit, he took a chaotic country that was living in the 18th century and transformed it into a modern nation. He built new roads, ports and factories, created jobs, and built up the economy. In short, he took a

*divine tropical island with an abundance of natural beauty
and wonder, and added commerce.*

*Sometimes you can get more done with a benevolent dicta-
tor than in a democracy, and certainly much faster. However,
it wasn't long before my eyes were opened to the truth. Once
he'd solidified his power, he began to use the National Guard
to terrorize and banish civilian opponents; there were rumors
of torture and even brutality.*

*The rumors of torture bothered me greatly, for I loved my
people, all of them, regardless of social status or political
affiliations. I loved my country. I am ashamed to say now, that
despite these feelings, I did little to investigate at that time.*

*About a year after we were married, the newspapers start-
ed to talk about this cute and adorable Rafael Leonidas
Trujillo Ramfis, the son Trujillo had with his wife, Maria
Martinez Alba in 1929 (Flor's half brother). Ridiculous as it
sounds the boy of four years old was named a Colonel in the
National Army and in 1938, at nine years old, was promoted
to brigadier general.*

*All of Trujillo's children were given appointments to pres-
tigious posts ranging from ambassador extraordinaire to honorary commandant of the army, mostly before they were ten
years old. No one ever voiced displeasure or disagreement, of
course. It was like the story of the Emperor Who Had No
Clothes.*

Because of his personality, Rubi could always depend upon a
certain "admiration" from Trujillo who was drawn to this man
who had a natural ability to accomplish what he, himself,
could only obtain through force.

Shortly after the marriage, Trujillo offered his new son-in-
law a position as Secretary of Legation in London, but Rubi
declined, citing his preference to remain in the country.
Instead, he was offered a job as president of the San Rafael
Insurance Company, which he took.

However, that turned out to be a very short stint, probably because it actually involved work. After that, he was appointed as a deputy to the Dominican congress, and again, that only lasted a few months before Rubi insisted on returning to the army. His wish was granted and he was given the rank of captain and Aide-de-Camp to the president.

Though Rubi was usually in the favor of Trujillo, in 1934 after being reinstated and after just two years of marriage, an incident gives us a glimpse into the couple's marriage:

One morning Flor practically tore down the door to her father's office. Her face was badly bruised as if she'd been hit, her clothes were disheveled, and she was out of breath.

"Look at what that animal has done to me, Father. Look at my eye!" Flor yelled. "I will not tolerate his violence. Father, you must punish him."

Though the bruise was extraordinary—the color of an eggplant, swollen and quite tender—her father looked at her coldly. He did not like to be interrupted, especially when he was conducting affairs of state and especially by his daughter. Several secretaries and aides were seated in the room.

After a moment's silence, however, he shouted into the other room, "Call Captain Rubirosa to my office immediately!"

Within the hour, Rubi arrived in Trujillo's office. The president was seated behind an enormous mahogany desk and Flor was standing, staring out the window. The aides sat with their heads bowed, keeping their gazes fixed on the floor as Porfirio stood at rigid attention. He saluted the president and then quickly spoke.

"Sir. I knew she would come here but I want you to know that I only hit her because she was disrespectful and that in my house, I am the man. I am the boss."

The room was silent. Rubi became tense. The president rose slowly from his chair and began to approach Porfirio. Aides turned their heads to the windows.

Finally, the president spoke. "You, you, and you, leave my office," he said, gesturing to the aides.

Flor seemed genuinely scared. The president brushed past Porfirio, crossed the room, and sat on a chair across from a small couch and table separating the two. Patting the couch softly several times, the president said, "Come. Come you two. My impetuous daughter and my hot-headed son-in-law. Let's discuss this problem."

Rubi let out an audible sigh and joined his wife across from the president. Half an hour later, Rubi and Flor left the office smiling broadly at each other and holding hands.

A friend of Rubi's burst out laughing several days later, when a friend of Flor's asked him, "Is it true that Rubi dared to strike Flor de Oro?" The man answered, "Hah, mention a single woman he hasn't hit."

This was probably the first published account of this kind of behavior, just one of the enigmas that was Porfirio Rubirosa. Rubi always stated emphatically that a man should never harm a woman. "Women don't like to be harmed; they love to be loved," he said.

He did later tell a friend that he had made a mistake that might have cost him his life, and he was appalled that this man (Trujillo) would allow his daughter to be struck without a reprisal.

Still further accounts much later appeared to counter his philosophy. The most publicized incident would occur in Paris in 1953 when Rubi was in his forties.

According to her book, *One Lifetime Is Not Enough*, Zsa Zsa Gabor, by then one of the loves of Rubi's life, recounted the incident:

"I first tasted the sting of Rubi's jealousy and felt the lash of his rage one night after we drove Prince Jimmy and Genevieve home to their house…

"…Rubi turned the key in the ignition, then suddenly, without warning, his eyes blazing like hot coals, slapped me hard in the side of the face. I screamed in shock. Genevieve came back out from the house and helped me out of the car. Without looking back, Rubi started the car and roared off into the heart of Paris.

"My nose was bleeding. I was hurt and humiliated, and let Genevieve lead me into one of the guest bedrooms, where I laid down. She was shaking and wringing her hands. 'How could he do this? I'm going to call the police,' she said.

"Suddenly, the doorbell rang. It was three in the morning. Genevieve implored me not to answer, knowing it was Rubi. I had no choice, Rubi owned me. I had lost my will. I was a part of him and I no longer belonged to myself...

"...He knelt in front of my bed and asked for my forgiveness. The next moment, we were making love, while I told myself, this can't be me. I'm married to George. I can't be this lost."

✗

In 1935, while still in the Army, Rubi became bored and decided to take his chances in the business world, his last attempt at legitimately "working" at any job.

It was a good opportunity for him to increase his income, and a better chance to escape the discipline and tedium of military service. He abhorred the monotony and the repetition, was not remotely interested in the Slavic devotion to authority, and he *hated* the food.

Until 1935, large ships coming into Santo Domingo went through an archaic routine. They had to drop anchor in the rough Caribbean Sea near the entrance to the Ozama River, and then, while they swayed and dipped with the large waves, they were unloaded onto barges. The barges rocked and wobbled in a similar fashion, so that the process of unloading was both dangerous and laborious. Many men were washed overboard during winter storms.

Once filled, the barges would then chug slowly up the

river, usually a half hour trip, until they could dock at small piers and once again be unloaded by teams of dockworkers.

Trujillo decided that a port should be built to allow for bigger ships and an increasing volume of imports. However, before a port could be constructed, the waters at the edge of the river would have to be dredged to accommodate the larger ships.

Rubi saw a chance to make a killing. He ordered a dredge from a company in New Orleans, planning to be the sole contractor in the operation.

While he waited three months for the dredge to arrive, another citizen, Benitez Rexach, an attorney with a close relationship to Trujillo, had the same idea and began undermining Rubi's efforts by telling the president that Rubi's dredge was dangerous, a steam-driven machine that could explode at any time.

Porfirio became so furious at the news that he threatened to kill Rexach, and the attorney took his predicament to the president who decided business was thicker than family blood. The contract was taken from Rubi and given to Rexach. The next week, Rubi was dispatched on yet another mission, a post in Berlin. The entrepreneurial effort cost him $100,000—the price of the dredge, and with that failure, went his hopes of becoming financially independent of his father-in-law.

He was furious, not only because it was the first time his father-in-law had undermined him, but because by then Porfirio—along with the rest of the country—was well aware of Trujillo's thievery. Using his political control of the nation, he was amassing great personal wealth. He had taken over plantations and businesses and given family, relatives, and political supporters lucrative jobs.

For the rest of Rubi's diplomatic career, he would be granted posts and then seemingly, have them withdrawn on

Trujillo's whims. The fact is that if Rubi's behavior caused the dictator embarrassment, he would promptly be dismissed. On the other hand, Rubi served a special purpose for Trujillo as no one else could, and so each time, at some point, he would find himself in the good graces of the dictator once again and would either receive a new appointment, or be reinstated to the previous one.

That same year, Rubi first appeared on the FBI's radar in New York.

According to FBI documents, file number NY-97-2078: "On April 28, 1935, a man named Sergio Bencosme, who often had expressed his opposition to the Dominican dictator Rafael Trujillo, was shot to death in New York, in an apartment he was sharing with Dr. Angel Morales, a leader of anti-Trujillo exiles in New York.

"Police later figured that Bencosme had been mistaken for Morales.

"Nearly a year later, a New York County grand jury indicted a man named Luis de la Fuente, Rubirosa (Rubi's cousin) for the murder.

"Luis Rubirosa had flown back to the Dominican Republic, where he was immediately made a lieutenant in the Dominican Army, though oddly, he had no previous record of military training.

"The State Department later asked the Trujillo government to find and produce him. They were told he was missing.

"Among Dominicans, it is generally thought that Rubirosa came to New York expressly to make arrangements for his cousin to assassinate Morales. Oddly, though Rubirosa travels frequently between the Dominican Republic and Europe, this is the first time he's dared to come to this country.

"The authorities in New York should now call Porfirio Rubirosa in for questioning with regard to the assassination of Dr. Sergio Bencosme."

In addition to that FBI document, we uncovered this information from confidential **State Department documents**:

"In 1935, Rubi traveled to Manhattan carrying a suitcase containing $7,000 in cash and arranged to have his cousin, Chi Chi de La Fuente Rubirosa, carry out a political assassination.

"The target was former Dominican minister, Dr. Angel Morales, a Trujillo political enemy living in exile in New York. However, the gunman botched the job, shooting Morales' roommate, Sergio Bencosme in the back. Morales and Bencosme were planning to return to Santo Domingo as candidates for president and vice president, respectively.

"They had the backing of the DuPonts who had made substantial loans to the country that Trujillo had neglected to repay. There were rumors that arms and munitions were being shipped to the Dominican Republic by the DuPonts by way of Mexico to aid in the overthrow of Trujillo.

"Chi Chi was eventually indicted, but not before he had been spirited back to the Dominican, having been made a lieutenant by a grateful Trujillo. When he demanded to be made a captain and threatened to talk, Rubi's cousin was also mysteriously killed."

'Honorary' Diplomat
Porfirio Rubirosa

THE term "playboy-diplomat" has been affixed to Porfirio Rubirosa for so many years that it may come as a surprise to some to realize that he is 52 years old. As a diplomat, Señor Rubirosa, known to millions of tabloid readers and a succession of five wives as Rubi, has evidently served the

Man in the News

Dominican Republic well enough to hold onto his diplomatic passport for twenty-five years. He was reported to be visiting the United States yesterday on a "private" mission of improving relations between the United States and the Dominican Republic.

However, Señor Rubirosa denied this and said that New York was merely a stopover on his way to Paris.

Even when he was attached to no particular embassy, Señor Rubirosa was an "honorary" diplomat, except for a brief period when he fell from favor with the Dominican Foreign Ministry because he was the co-respondent in two well-publicized divorce suits.

A rather full life .

All through my vagabond life, I had met men and women of diverse nationalities and ethnic groups that practiced a variety of religions and never were there any problems.

—Porfirio Rubirosa

Rubi wasted no time in putting the dredge fiasco behind him. An old proverb states that new doors don't open until old ones close, so Rubi gave up the entire enterprise, which proved to be an excellent choice.

Although he was angry with Trujillo, he needed money, so Rubi accepted a new appointment in 1936 as the Third Secretary of the Dominican Republic Legation to Berlin, just as Adolph Hitler began his reign of terror throughout the continent.

This diplomatic appointment proved to be the ignition for the fire of a notorious, if not illustrious, diplomatic career for Rubi that would last more than three decades. His Berlin post and subsequent other appointments hop-scotching around the world would give him entrée to the elite, super rich, celebrated, and some of the most dangerous people in the world.

In all, Porfirio Rubirosa held 13 different diplomatic posts during his lifetime, with titles as simple as Secretary of Legation, Paris, to the lofty moniker of Extraordinary Delegate and Minister Plenipotentiary in Rome. His career began in 1936 and ended in 1961 with his last post.

With his God-given, considerable capacity to charm and entertain everyone around him, diplomacy seemed the perfect calling. Back home Trujillo worded it a little differently: "He's an excellent diplomat because women like him, and because he's a great liar."

Before reporting to his post in Berlin, Rubi and Flor first went to Paris.

When I last left Europe, in 1928, peace seemed eternal. I was surprised at how much it had all changed. I had promised Flor I would open the doors of the evening and initiate her to the world of parties, but it was no longer the craziness of the "roaring '20s."

The great Argentinean orchestras and the American Jazz had been replaced with an odd mix of Gypsy and Russian groups.

The cabarets were still in fashion, however, ex-officers of the Czar's Imperial guard ran them. The most popular were Casanova, The Monsignor, and The Scheherazade.

The sound of the violins and the stomping of black boots, the guttural shouts of that syncopated music were both sentimental and nervous.

Under the artificial light of Montmarte, the Russian immigrants tried to recapture their nights in St. Petersburg. The air always seemed heavy with melancholy. They were sad, but also confident and warm.

In 1936, fifteen days after arriving in Europe, Rubi and Flor came into Berlin. World War II was officially still three years away, but Hitler was already in power and the city was filled with flags, banners, streamers, placards, and swastikas, most touting national socialism, not the Olympics.

The city seemed awash in an amazing air of pride, bordering on arrogance and superiority.

The laidback atmosphere of Paris—with its jazz clubs, cabarets, and easy lifestyle—with which Rubi was so enamored, was a distant memory. Here, in Berlin, it seemed that every gesture and expression was an odd mix of pride and a portent of war. Gone were the follies of the '20s. Talk was now of the popular front, strikes, and national pride.

Some things never change: the German women were just as interested in Rubi as the French, if not more so.

The Rubirosas' first stayed at the home of the Dominican Republic's minister. In addition, while Flor began searching the city for an apartment, Rubi was attending the Olympic Games on a daily basis and enjoying whatever adventures he could find at night. He rarely visited the embassy.

He was quickly becoming known as a dapper, mahogany-skinned, Latin polo player from "that" exotic distant Caribbean island.

Impeccably dressed at all times, he had a penchant for expensive Italian silk suits that draped over his body like that of a model. Even while playing polo, he was never without a silk scarf. When he did dress more casually, he often wore silk pants with expensive, soft leather, Italian loafers—probably the first man to dress in that manner without wearing socks.

Whether he was in a nightclub, lounging by a pool, or riding a pony, one could always smell just the right hint of his cologne and though his hair was naturally wiry, he wore it combed straight back with a touch of oil.

It wasn't long before Rubi met a young beauty in a bar, a woman who proved so engaging that he didn't arrive back at the minister's home until six a.m. the next morning—covered in lipstick—at which time he promptly went to bed and slept until noon.

A bouquet of a dozen red roses occupied his place setting at the luncheon table, along with a note and a torn, open envelope.

The minister and his wife were seated at the far end, and Flor sat to the side. All three were silent, but their expressions left nothing unsaid. Rubi could feel their disgust hanging in the air.

Rubi calmly pulled out his chair as if nothing had transpired, sat down, and began to read the note:

"Thanks great friend; thanks great, wonderful friend. In the Scandinavian countries, there is a summer night when the sun never sets. It is called St. John's night. You gave me yesterday, my first summer night."

A beautiful summer night was quickly turning into a harsh winter day.

Hell hath no furry, at least not like Flor's. Within days, their marriage began to teeter and in weeks, it was a foregone conclusion that Flor would ask for a divorce and return home at some point, but not before she pulled a revolver on him and threatened to shoot off the "leash" that was dragging him out to clubs.

A night did not pass that he wasn't out until dawn, returning disheveled and reeking of perfume. The German women were particularly fond of Latin American men because of their sexual reputations, and Rubi took every advantage of his heritage.

Flor was quoted as saying, "Whenever I asked him where he was, he would beat me."

Later that same year, Rubi was transferred to London in another diplomatic role as Secretary to the Mission representing the Dominican Republic, though he rarely worked and wasn't entirely sure what a Secretary to the Mission was.

He did manage to use his position and charm, however, to make friends with the Maharajah of Godwar, the Maharajah of Kapurthaia, and other dignitaries. One never knows when he will need a favor of a well-placed dignitary, either for the good of one's country or self.

It's very difficult to even speak about the Germany of 1936. Looking back now, the craziness only promised an apocalypse, which makes an objective tone difficult.

However, the Germany that I discovered that year was different. They were preparing for the Olympic Games. On the bronze bells of the stadium was engraved the slogan: "The National Socialism calls out to the youth of the world."

The pending games had attracted a colony of foreigners that frequented the bars of the great hotels. Blonde youths in uniforms marched in the streets—singing; playing guitars, accordions, and flutes. There were flags everywhere. People greeted each other by raising their thrusting fists into the air with an amazing pride.

The stadium was situated in the forest, and it rose majestically toward the sky awaiting the 150,000 spectators who would soon fill the stands.

By the first of August, I was going to the Games every day. One day, I was seated only a few meters away from Hitler. He was very animated and happy when a German won an event and ambivalent when someone else did.

I was frequently asked what effect Hitler had on me. I remember having mentioned to Flor one evening that he appeared ridiculous in motion pictures, but when you were near him, he gave off a certain power, a disquieting magnetism. One would forget his modest height and only remember his sparkling gaze, his self-willed mouth, and the abrupt movements of his hands.

Several weeks later, when the Games were over, I realized that the National Socialism Party was more than that. The realization came over me as a shock as I was near the station by the zoo.

Strolling one morning, I saw a pale man with straight black hair and a desperate look on his face. He was holding a book tightly over his heart. Suddenly, he moved and I noticed on the pocket of his dark vest, a yellow star with the word "Jude" in the center of it.

It shocked me. Racism had never occurred to me. In the Dominican, everyone was equal, black and white. There were social differences, but people of all classes frequented even the most elite clubs. Though many were poor, they wore their poverty lightly and evenly, always making the best of their situation.

We Dominicans always thought of ourselves as one big family, regardless of the differences in education, class, or race. I always loved my country for that.

The same held true in Paris where race was never an issue. I had an Israeli friend who had never appeared to me as being any different from the Protestants or Catholics. All through my vagabond life, I had met men and women of diverse nationalities and ethnic groups that practiced a variety of religions, and never were there any problems.

I've never known any race to have a monopoly on virtue or vice.

Seeing that young man labeled, almost as a cow is branded, jolted me, even made me nauseas. That moment, I became sensitive to the Jewish "problem" and I realized just how far the propaganda had gone. Everywhere I went from then on, at social gatherings, I would hear comments like, "He's a Jew." "His mother married a Jew"—things of that nature. For me, it was as if someone was ringing an alarm.

I was about to discover how much the Nazis despised the Jews. To their [way of] thinking, a Jew was just a parasitic vagabond.

It wasn't just the Jews that were being persecuted. For years, during the war, many outside Germany and Poland did not know what was happening. In fact, the gypsies, whose music had supplanted American Jazz in the cabarets, were being murdered as well. During the war, the Germans exterminated nearly 600,000 gypsies.

As the new secretary to the mission, Rubi was quickly learning about the perks of the diplomatic corps. In 1936, Rubi was asked to attend the coronation of George VI. It was there that he made many of his closest friends.

The British can be the most closed people in the world, but they can also be most cordial. Since I was now the Secretary to the Mission, a British consul received Flor and me at Dover. We were then escorted to London where I was given an enormous apartment in one of the best hotels, and a car was put at my disposal.

It was the occasion of the coronation of King George VI and the splendor of the British monarchy was in full regalia—true power that runs calm and deep from the strength of its history.

I will never forget how lavish it was. All the reigning princes of India, the Maharajah of Gackwarde-Baroda, the Maharajahs of Jaipur and Kapurthaia whom I became good friends with, and the many other dignitaries from around the world, were in attendance.

There were heavy brocade robes, satin and silk gowns, and it seemed everyone was literally dripping with jewels. There were ambassadors, kings, queens, and all manner of noteworthy people from the deserts, the virgin rain forests, and many eccentric and extraordinary surroundings—all were gathered at Westminster to witness the power of the British Empire.

I was presented to the majesties and the royal family at

Buckingham Palace where only the men were allowed. I felt a bit uncomfortable in the formal long-tailed coat, black socks, and spit-polished, black-pointed toe shoes, but I respected their traditions.

Later that day there was a naval review at Portsmouth, which brought to mind the same show of strength in Germany earlier that year, only that was a parade of tanks, large canons, and thousands of goose-stepping troops. This seemed somehow more dignified; certainly as confident.

Battleships, cruisers, and all types of supporting ships and boats passed by that day. If one ever doubted it, the fact that the British never lost a war because it always had supremacy of the seas was the real thing.

Their naval supremacy went back to Henry VIII, the king who loved so many women, sometimes cruelly. His life was dedicated to pleasure, sports, and creating the British fleet.

✗

Within months, Rubi was transferred yet again: This time he was to be the Counselor of Legation back in Paris, a role he relished because he had never been able to suppress his obsession with that city and its women.

Though he was still only 27, he had visions of reliving the adventures of his youth. Flor, who was aching to return home to the Dominican Republic, accompanied him begrudgingly.

It was with a great deal of pleasure that I found myself again in Paris, where I'd been named Consejero de la Legacion (Advisor to the Ambassador).

Flor and I lived in Neuilly along with an unwanted permanent guest, at least unwanted by me. It was Flor's cousin. She ate breakfast with us. She ate lunch and dinner with us. When I had to go to the embassy, she was glued to Flor's side, never leaving her for a second. If we went out at night, there she was as well.

She was even involved in all our arguments, which is not good for any couple. A man can generally convince one woman of the strength of his argument, but two is impossible. When a third person enters domestic disputes, things just get worse, especially one so subjective. She was not shy to begin with; now Flor had the added strength of an ally.

I remember one day having the worst argument we'd had since our wedding. Flor was always jealous, which didn't help things and aggravated my normally easygoing nature. Harsh words were thrown about in angry abandon. We both said things we knew we would regret.

Her cousin yelled at me from across the room, "Porfirio Rubirosa (she always referred to me by my entire name when she was angry, which was most of the time), they are preparing a bed of ashes for you in hell." By "they," I assumed she meant the devil and his disciples.

To top it all off, she was a horror to behold. Her skin was like the husk of something washed up at high tide, then left for a month in the hot sun—as brittle as a new soda cracker.

I thought of her as a witch, which always reminded me of how in early America, in Salem, when someone was suspected of being a witch, they would throw them into a river or lake. If they floated, they were witches. If they submerged and drowned, well they drowned. I wanted to tie her to the anchor of a boat and pitch her in the Seine.

Flor's cousin only stoked the flames by pouring on more fuel. She would say to Flor, "I just don't understand how you let yourself be treated in this manner, Flor. After all, you are the daughter of President Trujillo. How can you permit a man to speak to you in that manner, the daughter of the Benefactor, even if he is your husband?"

Until the arrival of her cousin, Flor and I only experienced the normal disagreements that most couples have, the ones where a wife wants to have exclusive rights and the husband is perhaps a bit wayward.

I always felt love could cure all wounds. If there is love, it is important to communicate, to give and take. Disagreements of this type should not be that serious.

"You have to teach him a lesson," I could hear her saying in the other room. "I am going home to Santo Domingo and you should accompany me. Just make up some excuse. When you've put some time and distance between you, you'll see into your heart and you'll be able to judge if you can continue a life like this; certainly not the life of the daughter of President Trujillo."

Wanting a divorce, but not wanting a struggle, Flor made up an excuse to return home—her father needed her desperately to help with important family business, she said. However, as she left the city, she dropped a letter in a mailbox admitting to Rubi that the story was a lie. She only needed to see if she could live without him and the only way to do that was to put a great body of water between them.

It wasn't long after her return to the Dominican Republic, however, that Flor changed her mind and asked Rubi's mother to intervene by writing her son, telling him that Flor loved him, wanted him to forgive her, and to come and get her.

Rubi received the letter, but chose to ignore it. His decision was made easier because Trujillo had passed a law allowing couples to divorce if, in five years of marriage, they had borne no children. It is important to note here that the infertility which rendered the couple childless was not Flor's problem—Rubi was sterile—just one more detail of particular interest to the women who loved him.

After the divorce, Rubi was informed by the Dominican minister in Paris that his duties had been suspended and that Trujillo had publicly declared him a "persona non grata" for divorcing his daughter—none of which bothered Rubi much. He was an ocean away and increasingly more grateful for it, especially when rumor reached Europe that his ex-father-in-law had just committed genocide.

Trujillo's most notorious act was committed against his island neighbor, Haiti. Trujillo had always made it clear that he held racist ideas and considered the dark-skinned Haitians to be inferior. In 1937, he took action to resolve this problematic issue by giving the order to his army to massacre all Haitians found to be in the Dominican Republic. He referred to them as "squatters."

Estimates of as many as 17,000 to 20,000 unarmed Haitian men, women, and children were slaughtered in a blood bath of violence, particularly around the border region of the town of Dajabon and the aptly named "Massacre River."

When I learned of the massacre, I was sickened beyond belief, but just as I could do nothing about my friends the Jews, I was helpless to exact any change at home.

I must admit with some shame now, I did not suffer long. The freedom in Paris had always been agreeable to me and I quickly masked my disgust by frequenting Jimmy's, a small "boite."

What a great burden of guilt men have. We gather our arms around it, while at the same time, we go on as if nothing were happening. What other choice did I have?

It is easier to look the other way, when you are removed from the reality by thousands of miles of ocean and the frivolity of the atmosphere in Paris.

Jimmy's had an excellent orchestra and the place was always filled with rich Nordic students. They used to let me sit in and play the guitar or the drums and to sing occasionally.

The Nordic female students were particularly pleasing and we would often party through the night, into the morning, and up until noon.

Even though he was only 28, Rubi was already gaining a reputation for what would later be recounted dozens of times, through as many perspectives, as shall we say, "Being well endowed." Perhaps so endowed physically that no less than the likes of Truman Capote and *Vanity Fair* magazine reported on this phenomena.

In his novel, *Answered Prayers*, Capote described Rubi's principal endowment as an "eleven-inch café-au-lait sinker as thick as a man's wrist."

And, according to *Vanity Fair*, December 2002, "Rubi's constant state of erection earned him the nickname, *Toujours Pret*, which when translated into English is the motto of the U.S. Coast Guard: 'Always ready.'"

When asked to compare Rubi's member to a certain writer's size 11 shoe, one of his paramours glanced at the shoe and merely shrugged, saying, "Rubi was bigger.'"

On a final Flor de Oro note in this regard: Flor did not leave any written history of her marriage to Rubi. However, many years later in 1975, after she had died, a friend of hers found an audiotape account of her life with Rubi. In it, Flor described what had happened the first night of their honeymoon:

"I was still wearing my wedding dress so that my mother (Trujillo's first wife, who was not invited by Trujillo to the wedding) could see it before I lost my virginity. Porfirio took me to the nuptial bed. I was scared—this 'thing' lurching at me! I was disgusted and became afraid, running all over the house."

Flor said she was sore for a week after that first night.

Perhaps it occurred with puberty, given his propensity for womanizing even in his early years in Paris. However,

Rubi was either blessed or cursed (depending on your out-look) with an affliction known as priapism. Most say it wasn't his sexual prowess that made him so irresistible to women—rather, it was his utter devotion to them—many would agree his "endowment" certainly did not hinder him.

Men who have this disorder report various levels of problems ranging from merely annoying to excruciating pain.

Essentially, priapism is a prolonged and painful erection that can last from several hours up to a few days. The erection *is not* necessarily the result of sexual thoughts or stimulation, but it *is* an inability for blood to drain out of the penis.

Most men think they would welcome just such a problem. However, if the condition lasts for more than a few hours, since the penis provides little room for blood to circulate, the blood becomes stagnant after a while and then acidifies and loses oxygen. Without oxygen, the red blood cells become stiff and even less able to drain.

This is enough of a predicament for the average male; however, Rubi's penis was reported to be eleven inches long, with significant girth—so much so that in later years the waiters in Parisian restaurants began referring to the giant peppermills as "Rubirosas," a name that has survived to this day.

For Rubi, who so loved women, one can see how he was torn. He knew that when he was aroused, he would most certainly remain erect for hours and even days, which was quite painful.

One can only imagine the discomfort, both physically and emotionally, of having to live with, and in some cases, hide his endowment.

The "curse" not only involved pain, but also the fact that once erect he had great difficulty achieving orgasm. Therefore, it is surmised that because of his devotion to women, he considered his affliction a gift he was more than willing to share.

In the book, *Too Rich: The Family Secrets of Doris Duke* (Pony Duke and Jason Thomas), about one of Rubi's later marriages, Duke and Thomas describe Rubi's anatomy and the subject of sex among the rich and famous.

"The length, both in times of passion and in times of repose, was always in excess of eleven inches. At all times, it was six inches in 'circumference' not, as erroneous accounts reported, six inches in diameter.

"The best description is that it was much like the last foot of a Louisville Slugger baseball bat, with the consistency of a not completely inflated volleyball.

"Doris Duke believed that the very rich and the very poor often have the same attitude toward great sex. The very rich can buy almost anything except a perfect climax, so when this joyous event occurs, it is vastly appreciated.

"The very poor have nothing, so when they have the opportunity to experience great sex, it is wondrous.

"For those two opposites of the social spectrum, sex can be more important than anything. More important than jobs, mortgages, college tuitions, or a new living room set. Being poor or rich gives a person a freedom of sexual indulgence that usually escapes the middle classes."

Rubi marries French movie star Danielle Darrieux

Some of the best gigolos are, like Rubirosa, products of such countries as Italy, Spain, Greece, and Latin America where a boy is brought up surrounded and spoiled by women—mother, sisters, aunts. He learns quickly how to please them. Physical communication such as kissing and hugging is ordinary and natural and lovemaking is demystified at an early age....

– Lynn Ramsey, *Gigolos*

A playboy is a squandering type. He only thinks of fun, adventure, and living in "sprees." He despises work or serious responsibilities. He likes his freedom, independence, and an easy way of life.

In a way, he loves a woman's money, but does not love a wealthy woman only for her money.

He is inclined to partake in luxury and hardly ever considers death or other such abstract matters. This is the life of a playboy, which can easily evolve into a restless and indolent career.

To a confirmed playboy, considering marriage would be like following the stock market from death row. What's the point? From the playboy's point of view, marriage takes much out of a man, is an enormous drain on his time, and produces continual deficits (in my case, just the opposite was true).

It is said that there are three advantages to playing the field: One, you can think. Two, you can act; and three, you can feel.

A woman has the tendency to twist a man's life to her own ends, and never so vividly as in marriage. She can fill his nights with anxiety, and erase his peace of mind so that he barely remembers that blessed feeling.

I will always remember my friend Alajandro's words: "To Rubi, marriage is a train wreck for a man. It filets his soul one tiny piece at a time, then broils it until nothing remains but a hank of hair and the harness he wore."

Some men should have two lovers and others should have three. It simply depends on each individual's level of energy. However, under no circumstances should one ever limit himself to a monogamous relationship.

Having more than one lover does present scheduling problems, however, which can test even the best organizational skills of any man.

Ahh, living alone in a cushy apartment or small villa is ideal. Your friendly Swedish housekeeper comes in every Friday to put a buff on things; the corner laundry delivers your crisply pressed shirts; and your lady friends stop by, preferably by appointment, anxious and thrilled at the prospect of pleasing you—their eyes lighting up at the very sight of you, their lips flush and moist, with the radiance of desire glowing on their cheeks.

My married friends argue with me constantly, saying, "No woman would ever accept an arrangement like that." Or, "It would be impossible to lie to three women at once. This is all far too selfish of you."

I reply, Yes. I am selfish, but only because I have a greater capacity for pleasure than most men. To others, pleasure is a part-time diversion. To me, it is a vocation.

Picture yourself in my situation. You are eating a sumptuous meal with a ravishing young lady with a vivacious tongue, who though she adores you, argues politics and ideas, which of course, you care nothing about. However, you are enjoying the banter, knowing that in a few hours, you will be happily lying next to her as she nuzzles you with that drowsy smile, and you end the evening in each other's embrace, thoroughly spent, yet filled with anticipation of who will visit tomorrow.

By definition, a gigolo is different, if only for one word associated with the playboy—rich. Generally speaking, the gigolo is seeking fortune along with the pleasures and lack of responsibility.

Wealthy society spawned playboys, but it was originally "dance" that gave birth to the gigolo. In the early 1900s, the word referred to an elegant young man whose lifestyle and means were somewhat dubious, specifically the professional dancing partner who had glided into society on the coattails of that prewar craze, the tango.

The tango had begun as a rough and tumble peasant dance in the sleazy watering holes of the Argentina coast (the location of yet another diplomatic post, later for Rubi).

Rubi was attracted to the rhythms, which were both sensuous and nearly violent, but it was the lyrics that really captivated him. The language of the tango had its roots in a medieval religious concept that considered women as diabolical creatures whose purpose was to incite men to sin in sexual ways. The inhabitants of Buenos Aires first adopted these lyrics and rhythms, and Rubi was irresistibly drawn to all of it.

Around 1911, the Parisians were the first people outside South America to adopt the tango, and although they refined its violent movements so that ultimately it became a graceful, aristocratic amusement, the gigolo's image always retained the flavor of the tango's lowly origins—and his own. He was first a dance partner, then a professional escort—then, a fortune hunter.

Certainly, Porfirio Rubirosa was the ultimate playboy; and there is no denying he hated work, but Rubi appeared far more faceted than a mere gigolo or playboy. He truly loved the women he romanced even as he spoke of marriage as a yoke, he did ultimately fall prey to love and subsequently married five times, but he never stopped loving others at the same time.

When he was with a woman, nothing else mattered. Her money meant nothing to him. Nothing could distract him from lavishing his attention and true affections upon her. It appears that more than anything, he just happened to be attractive and alluring enough, that the wealthy, and perhaps more confident and aggressive women were attracted to *him*. If they happened to possess a fortune, Rubi never held that against them.

According to Bob Williams, a columnist who once asked Rubi what his secret to success was with women, Rubirosa replied, "It is such an easy trick: All I do is maintain eye contact and appear to be unaware of any other woman—any other person—in the room. Intense concentration is my secret weapon."

In reality, it isn't a trick. I was always sincere, because I could never get enough, but I never let that be known. And I never chased women. In the beginning, whether I was seated alone at a sidewalk café, or in a booth at a club, I was quite aloof. There is something about disinterest that drives women crazy.

However, once they approached me, I gave my heart and soul to them. I listened intently, always maintaining eye contact and a bit of a smile—an empathetic smile, I called it. I rarely spoke of myself, and that is important.

When I said to a woman: My love, you are the light of my life. I want to know everything, every detail about you. What champagne do you love? Do you sleep in the nude? What is your favorite book? Share with me what is in your heart and your soul so that I can be whole—I meant it, but of course, that is a difficult level of attention to maintain over the long haul.

I knew married men who were miserable, mostly because they never paid attention to their wives; to what they were saying; to what they wanted.

"Why don't we ever talk to each other?" That is the question most wives ask their husbands.

"Why don't we ever make love anymore?" That is the second question most wives ask their husbands.

Perhaps all this is borne of familiarity—too many days together, too privy to each other's every movement and thought. I don't know. I never stayed that long.

Although Rubi, the lover, would go on to become an adventurer, a sunken treasure hunter, a financier, a spy, a race car driver and almost a movie star, he was always astute enough to take advantage of every opportunity that presented itself.

Regardless of the many monikers he wore, one thing was constant. His only true loyalty outside the women he loved was his country.

No matter where he traveled or what celebrity he befriended, his heart always remained in the Dominican Republic. Perhaps his only despair was the atrocities of his ex-father-in-law.

In addition to being a thief, stealing most of the property in the Dominican, and murdering thousands of people, Trujillo was the worst kind of pedophile—he routinely had young girls kidnapped, then raped them and had them disposed of.

At some point, Rubi, knowing this, must have felt a deep darkness. The truth of Rubi could be found somewhere between his desire for frivolous adventures and his disdain and hatred for what Trujillo was doing to his country.

Between 1937 and 1938, after Flor left, and just before the War, for the first time in his life, Rubi discovered poverty and despair, two bedfellows to which he did not take kindly. He was unemployed and ostracized, at least at home, by Trujillo. Indeed, he couldn't even return home because at that point, his ex-father-in-law would have had him killed.

I was floundering a bit, I suppose. I had no job and was single again, not that playing at diplomacy paid much; it was the power and the prestige and the convenience that made it all so appealing, and women always love a man in a position of power, because, for one thing, you don't get there without a great deal of innate confidence, which is so appealing to women.

However, my loss of status, my sudden poverty, did not change my habits and women were still very attracted to me. In fact, I remember celebrating my new freedom one evening with a woman named Rene. She could have cared less if I were royalty or the junkman. She simply adored sex with me.

One night while we sat at Jimmy's, I told her: There is a bottle of champagne that will turn on the porch lights in your eyes, and a few dozen oysters waiting at my place. (I loved to talk of love in preparation for it.)

My dear, when we get there, I will pull a large chilled steel bowl from the refrigerator and make us an enormous salad with basil, spinach, fennel, cilantro, and radicchio, and we'll cover it with extra virgin olive oil and just a few drops of vinegar.

When we've finished that, I will prepare for us, steak tartare with chopped onions and an egg yolk.

Then, we will undress each other rapidly, without shame, as the adults we are, and jump into my big bed and tease each other as only childish adults can.

Then, after we are spent, I will prepare for us an omelet such as you have never tasted, and then we'll jump back into bed again, eat it there, and then make love for an hour—maybe more.

She squeezed my hand and I could feel her pulse in it. She smiled and I said, My dear beautiful girl, this is the best time of year for oysters, and we should never eat them without erotic plans afterward.

Though unemployed at the age of 29, Rubi used his guile and unique talents to entertain women, along with a healthy dose of shrewdness to survive and even flourish.

At first, he concocted a plan to sell Dominican Republic visas to Jews who were frantically trying to flee Europe. His home also seemed the best destination for these people.

Oddly enough, though Trujillo was known for torturing and murdering his own people, during the late '30s, he gained international attention for his open policy of allowing Jewish emigration from Europe, even encouraging it, while larger and wealthier nations were turning back Jewish refuges. Perhaps this is where many of Rubi's Dominican passport-carrying immigrants fled.

Neither the U.S. nor any other Western democracy really wanted the Jews. Senator Claiborne Pell said that at first Hitler did not want to kill the Jews—he just wanted to be rid of them. "But," said Pell, "the only country in the Western hemisphere that would take them was the Dominican Republic."

Some historians regard Trujillo's gestures as little more than public relations ploys. Others say it was an attempt to "whiten" the predominantly mixed race nation. Oddly, though he was of mixed ancestry, it was said Trujillo wore makeup to give himself a whiter appearance.

It was also thought that the "whitening" of the country meant the addition of the kind of intelligence and business acumen that Trujillo perceived the Jewish population might add.

Selling passports helped Rubi to support himself for a short time with this enterprise, charging them anywhere from $300 to $3,000 depending upon how much baggage they carried.

He was making money and ingratiating himself to many important, wealthy people. However, he might have ultimately had a more altruistic motivation.

Rubi had started this enterprise as simply a way to make money, once he learned of Trujillo's intentions, Rubi's initiative began to look similar to the story of *Schindler's List*, made so famous through the Steven Spielberg movie.

Knowing how deeply Rubi was struck by the discrimination while in Germany, it is not inconceivable that he was eventually driven to save lives by helping these people travel to his homeland. He knew that Trujillo valued their talents and intelligence and that they would therefore be safe.

He may have played a vital role in creating a complete Jewish community in the Dominican Republic, regardless of what his ex-father-in-law's intentions were. The community of Samana still exists to this day, and is thriving, as it always did.

However, this point in history was not recorded in the Dominican Republic in the same manner. According to an interview with Bonaparte Gautreaux Pineiro, the former head of the Domincan Republic's National Drug Counsel and Enforcement Office, and also a respected journalist, novelist, Dominican historian., and a staunch anti Trujillo commentator:

"Rubirosa did not save Jews. In times of Trujillo, all this was done by express disposition of the Superiority (Trujillo).

"In this case, this was not Rubirosa's initiative. He was following orders.

"When the Jewish persecution started, the majority of countries closed their doors. Trujillo saw a good opportunity to be presented as a benefactor.... It was a PR move to change the perception that he had ordered the murder of thousands of Haitians in 1937."

During this time (1938), Rubi met a beguiling young woman,

a French singer, La Mome Moineau, who also happened to be the wife of Benitez Rexach, the engineer who had cheated Rubi in the dredging swindle in Santo Domingo.

La Mome wasn't a rich heiress, she was a cabaret singer. However, she had gotten lucky when she met Rexach, who provided her with a luxurious home, a fleet of expensive cars, and a yacht. Oddly enough, he had no reservations about leaving her alone in Paris, while business dictated he live in Santo Domingo.

Her outrageous shopping sprees and party nights are what ultimately brought her into the arms of Rubirosa and in the final analysis, it was her jewels that came to his rescue—in fact, they saved him from financial collapse.

However, it wasn't just La Mome's jewels that bailed him out of poverty—it was an additional opportunity that serendipitously presented itself, that really catapulted him. This time in his life became known as Rubi's "precious stones" period.

In late 1938, a jeweler and an exile from the Spanish Civil War named Aldao, approached Rubi for help. In Aldao's haste to leave the country, he said he had left behind a fortune in rubies, sapphires, diamonds, and pearls, all sealed in a safe in his store in Madrid.

Knowing that Rubi still possessed diplomatic credentials and could therefore come and go without being searched by customs, he asked Rubi for help in retrieving the bounty—for a reward, of course.

His harrowing story captivated Rubi. According to Aldao, there were five velvet-lined, ornate, jewel-encrusted boxes all neatly piled in a large wall safe hidden in the basement.

"Neither the government nor the rebels will ever find it. They are too stupid," he said. "Besides, it is hidden behind a false bookshelf, and it is made of case-hardened steel three inches thick.

"I narrowly escaped, just seconds before the rebels began

to pillage the stores on the block. They were taking anything of value: jewels, paintings, silk embroidery, everything that wasn't nailed down. Anyone who was found in the storefronts was unceremoniously shot.

"It will be easy for you because they are now camped outside the city, and I will give you the combination to the safe."

At first, the plan seemed simple to Rubi. He would borrow the Dominican Minister's car and private chauffeur and drive to Madrid, a distance of about 400 miles, circumvent the rebel's encampment several miles from town, and then retrieve the jewels, bring them back, and receive his compensation from Aldao.

However, just before he was to depart, another man approached Rubi with a similar story, saying he also had $160,000 in cash and jewelry hidden in Madrid. His name was Johnny Kohane, a large heavyset Polish man, and he insisted on traveling with Rubi, who agreed, assuming this would add to his commissions.

Kohane was given the chauffeur's credentials and the two embarked on their secret mission across France and into Spain.

Apparently, the addition of this second player gave Rubi a different idea. Several days later, he returned to the Legation minus the Polish passenger. When questioned about the disappearance of his traveling companion, Rubi related his harrowing story:

"Someone must have been tipped off. We had hundreds of thousands of dollars worth of jewels in satchels in the trunk. Kohane was driving, and I sat in the backseat.

"Somewhere along those winding roads outside Guadalajara, where the bluffs and cliffs can hide an army, we were attacked with a hail of bullets by snipers—roadside bandits, I suppose. The cacophony sounded like a combination of rifles and automatic weapons.

"Johnny pulled the car off the road behind some large rocks and we made a run for it. I jumped out of the backseat, opened the trunk, and grabbed both leather satchels, each sealed with a heavy brass lock. Johnny had one key, I had the other.

"The bullets were ricoching off the rocks and splashing up sand around me as I rolled with the bags behind a large boulder. Johnny went in the opposite direction across the road and disappeared into the hills.

"After some time, the sound of rifle fire ceased and I returned to the car, but Johnny was nowhere to be found. My first thought was that they must have captured, perhaps killed him.

"Fearing for my own life, I sped off on the road to Saragossa and didn't look back, as you might well understand."

Later, when the Minister checked the car, he could find no evidence of an attack. The car appeared to be untouched, without a single bullet hole or scratch. The Minister and the others in the Legation simply accepted Rubi's story as just another of those strange but common mysteries that seemed to occur during Trujillo's era. Kohane was never heard from again.

Rubi did come home with jewels, which he kept in a royal blue velvet bag with a gold drawstring. When he handed it over to Aldao, Aldao opened it, gave Rubi a questioning look, and then gently hoisted the bag into the air several times.

"Senõr Rubirosa, the bag seems very light," he said. "And there is no inventory list from my assistant in Madrid, as I requested you obtain."

"Aldao, I hope you are not suggesting what I think you are," Rubi answered defiantly.

The merchant had no alternative. He couldn't prove what he'd left in the safe and so was obliged to not only take a loss, but to pay Rubi the eight diamonds promised for his services.

Months later, Aldao was able to prove his contentions. More than $180,000 worth of gems were missing, but a letter of complaint to the Dominican Legation in care of Rafael Trujillo proved fruitless. The incident was closed.

No one knows if Rubi also found Kohane's supposed stash of jewels. If he had, and they were indeed worth $160,000, that gave Rubi a tidy bankroll of $340,000, the equivalent of $5,000,000 in today's dollars.

After that, it was public knowledge that Rubi had turned his bad fortunes around. He began to squander money in 1938, and he was rapidly gaining attention and popularity as a big spender at restaurants and nightclubs.

He would dine with several women at a time, ordering only the finest champagne, caviar, and desserts, and leave tips larger than the tabs. Dancing the night away in fine new silk suits and handmade Italian leather shoes, he would practically throw money at the bandleaders after each frenetic piece.

Along with his patronizing and squandering ways came an increased popularity and awareness of this rich Latin playboy.

To lend credence to this story, a then classified FBI document stated:

"The files of Emilio Morel, former Dominican Ambassador to Spain, now living in New York, showed that Rubirosa had a Pole named Johnny Kohane with him when he left Paris to bring back the gems secreted by a friend for Manuel Fernandez Aldao, a Madrid jeweler who had fled to France.

"Rubirosa arranged false credentials for Kohane, and a curtain of mystery covers the events following their entering war-torn Spain.

"It is reported that 10 or 12 days later, Rubirosa returned from his journey to Madrid and said he and Kohane left Madrid with the securities. On the way, they were intercepted by men who fired upon Kohane, who was killed.

"Rubirosa stated he only had time to save his own life and did not notify authorities. Before leaving for Madrid,

Rubirosa was in a very poor financial position, but after his return, he embarked upon a life of extravagance, with talk of going into the cabaret business."

This particular story was perhaps the first incident that I read about in my research that convinced me Rubi was much more than just a gigolo. It also suggested that Rubi had long since realized the powers he had as a diplomat and that he rarely appeared to "work" at it. In fact, that is precisely what he was doing, at least in the sense that he used his immunity and ability to travel extensively, for his own agenda as well as Trujillo's.

In 1939, for reasons more apparent this time, Trujillo had once again warmed to Rubi and contacted him in Paris by phone asking if Rubi would take care of his wife, Maria, and his 10-year old son, Ramfis, as a sort of guide—help them find a home and entertain them. They would be arriving shortly in Paris. Maria was pregnant as well.

Rubi took great care to tend to Maria and Ramfis, fearing Trujillo's ulterior motives. Maria wrote back to her husband giving Rubi glowing reports and within the next month, Trujillo himself was on his way to Paris.

It was about a year after divorcing Flor. I didn't expect, nor did I receive any correspondences from Trujillo.

I was just waking up around noon after another night at Jimmy's, when the telephone rang. The operator said it was a call from Santo Domingo. I immediately thought something was wrong with my mother. Instead, I heard a strange voice say, "Rubirosa, I have the President standing here with me. He wants to know if you can attend to his wife and son who will be arriving in Paris in a few weeks.

"You would have to find them a house and accompany them around the city." Then there was silence. I was dumb-

founded and could not answer right away. At first, I thought it was a trap of some sort. What might be hidden in his proposition? Throughout the many times he'd hired and fired me, I usually knew the reasons—either I'd embarrassed him in the eyes of the world, or he had an agenda of his own, wherein I served some purpose for him. Ours was an odd symbiotic relationship, but by then, I'd grown to fully despise him.

I thought for another moment. I couldn't see the harm and since the Generalissimo hostilities had put me out of work, which was causing me problems, I accepted.

Maria Martinez Alba, Mrs. Trujillo, arrived later with the son she'd had with Trujillo in 1929. His name was Ramfis. She was also pregnant. In fact, so much so that I had to find a hospital the day she arrived. It was the American Hospital of Neuilly and Maria de Los Angeles, del Corazon de Jesus was born.

After Maria and the baby left the hospital, she wrote to her husband and gave me a glowing report. "Mr. Rubirosa is enchanting and polite." She relayed to me that he was thankful. One month later, he also arrived in Paris.

I did not know what to make of it. Even though I'd been kind and helpful to his wife and child, I suspected he might still be the fuming ex-father-in-law—an autocrat exasperated by my impertinence—just lying in wait to punish me.

Instead, to my great surprise, I found him agreeable and friendly, like he could be when he wanted to—though in my heart I could only think of what a pig and a murderer he was. For yet another time, I found myself filled with guilt about my relationship with this man.

The first words out of his mouth were, "Porfirio, do not leave my side." I could see the smiles disappear off his aides' faces, knowing that they would not be seeing the Parisian nightlife now that I was in the picture.

"Let's ditch these people," he whispered to me. "I want

you to show me everything. You know what I mean? Everything."

He knew no more about the Paris nightlife than a greyhound dog knows of internal combustion.

To me, that meant all the elegant places, anywhere without rice and beans. For some reason, the Eiffel Tower attracted him more than anything, so I took him to the top platform. There, he met a postcard salesgirl who was fresh, enchanting, and a bit trashy in her very short skirt and cheap perfume. Trujillo could have courted any number of topnotch, well-known ladies while in Paris, but he was absolutely smitten by this very young woman-practically a girl.

He kept repeating, "This Parisian girl at the highest spot in Paris is formidable," meaning of course that he wanted to have sex with her right then and there. He asked for my help and I obliged. Apparently, the thought of having raw sex with this girl, right out in the open, with the added danger of being found, was quite stimulating to him.

Knowing the Tower as well as I did, I knew the safest spot would be at the very top. The second floor is about 115 meters high—about the height of a 30-story building. From there, you can take one of three elevators to the top, which is about 250 meters high, about 75 stories.

The second floor is quite busy, but at the top, there are often times when no one is around. The view, as you might imagine, is spectacular—a 360-degree breathtaking vista of all of Paris.

After performing a perfunctory introduction, the young nubile girl was all smiles and Trujillo acted as a dog in heat, nearly panting with anticipation as I put the two of them on the elevator to the top.

When they returned to the second floor about 20 minutes later, the girl was disheveled, her hair a jumble of tangles, her blouse askew as she tried to tuck it back into her skirt.

The relationship had obviously been consummated; perhaps not without a bit of roughness. She did not smile, he was *beaming like a jackal fresh off a kill, satiated, its stomach full to bursting.*

I'm not proud of what I did. All I could think of were all the young girls back home that had disappeared.

After that, I was named Person in Charge of Business for the Dominican Republic in Paris. I think the tyrant was running low on titles for me by this time.

After bestowing this new rubric on me, he promptly sent home all of his entourage, including ministers, generals, and secretaries and we went to Bourboule, accompanied only by his doctor and a Colonel MacLaughlin.

There, we luxuriated in the spa, but Trujillo quickly grew bored. Then he asked to see Biarritz, where he was most impressed with the Hotel Du Palais. He even asked to see the blueprints, intent on building a similar place in Santo Domingo. In fact, the President seemed to want to replicate half of Paris somehow in Santo Domingo. He particularly loved Jimmy's.

"We need a Jimmy's in Santo Domingo," he said. "Only it needs to have four orchestras, not just one, and we need gardens and an entrance to the beach."

He then ordered his ship, the Ramfis, to the Mediterranean. On board, he planned an excursion to Egypt for us.

"Porfirio, it will be your job to direct this trip," he told me.

Okay. First stop, Cannes. Trujillo was beside himself—women everywhere, a never ending flow of champagne, a warm soft sun, and waters as blue as those of our homeland. To him, it was paradise.

One morning, as we cruised the Mediterranean en route to our next stop, a crewmember gave Trujillo the day's newspaper. The headline read simply, "General Mobilization."

In less than a minute, the President's demeanor completely changed; gone were the relaxed smile and the slow, easy breathing. He jumped to his feet and yelled, "It's war! We need to return immediately to Santo Domingo."

When the ship had returned, Trujillo ordered me to stay with his wife and two children, telling me he would return home alone immediately and send for his family later.

What had scared him so? Perhaps he thought that the war would debilitate his power.

Later, I accompanied Trujillo's family to Havre, where they departed for home safely.

Those early days in Paris seemed like a game. In spite of the daily reports in the papers and all the speeches, no one seemed to believe in the imminence of a violent conflict. I began to be more concerned about Hitler than the atrocities at home.

Hitler occupied Moravia and Slovakia and had renounced the nonaggression pact with Poland and a naval agreement with England. Everyone should have prepared himself. Germany also withdrew from a 10-year alliance with Italy and a nonaggression pact with the U.S.S.R.

England was building radar stations to thwart enemy attacks and launching huge weather balloons as barriers against aircraft. They were getting ready; France wasn't.

The French blithely thought we were in a mobilization period in which everyone would be counting troops, arms, restoring factories, and preparing tanks—and whoever had the most on paper, would win the war. In addition, since the capitalist countries were stronger and richer than the Third Reich, we could all soon consider ourselves the winners, they thought.

After May of 1940, we would no longer feel the same. I was caught up in the exodus, first to Tours, then to Bordeaux. Our cars were filled with staff and files.

I started out covering only 20 kilometers the first two days because we were not traveling the main roads. I'm not very sensible during times of drama and it was impossible for me not to show a great deal of emotion toward this country that I loved, the country that had won during the First World War. Was this going to be the Second?

The French were totally unprepared—I would say, nearly oblivious to what was coming, not only because of the political structure but also because of their very nature.

What was amazing about this exodus in June 1940 was the impotency of this great country to work collectively during this disaster. Nothing was prepared, particularly the hearts and minds of the people.

The individual and the society had been stretched beyond their limits. Their giving up was one of the saddest periods of my life.

I knew some friends were waiting for me in Biarritz. Officially, the Dominican de Legation should have occupied a castle near St. Emilio, so I went there and found several refugees.

It was at St. Jean de Luz where I first saw the German troops. There was a column of young blonde men with rosy cheeks. They sang as they marched. It seemed like the end of the world.

France was occupied, and without a shot being fired, as far as I could tell. It was the end. You could still drink, but you couldn't get drunk. Women's laughter seemed either forced or nearly hysterical.

The French became accustomed to defeat very fast.

In 1940, the German occupation in Paris brought about the creation of the Vichy Government: Frenchmen sympathetic to the Nazis, or at least too fearful to fight them. As a result, the Chamber and Senate had to move together with the diplomatic corps to the capital. I returned to Paris and then went on to Vichy. Paris, Vichy, Vichy to Paris, this was my itinerary in the fall of 1940. La Mome traveled with me.

During that time, a friend invited me to a cocktail party. I was still a diplomat and I had my own car and when it was time to leave, another friend approached me and introduced me to a beautiful young girl named Danielle Darrieux, who asked if I would escort her home.

Of course, I quickly replied.

"Be careful," a friend of mine whispered to her. "This man's dangerous."

"Really?" she said, with a wry laugh.

She gave me her address and by coincidence, her house was next to mine, though I'd never seen her before that party. I simply took her home and walked her to her door, and we said goodbye. I remember not being particularly struck by her, other than that she was quite attractive—I had no idea she was an actress.

Some time later, in L'aigion, I was seated at a table not far from her. I'd been told she was going through a divorce, but she was sitting with her husband.

Without knowing a single sentence of their relationship, I could see why she would want to divorce him. He was an angry man with an angry face. His eyebrows were pulled down so that the skin from his temples narrowed his eyes so closely together, he appeared nearly cyclopean. Perhaps they were fighting, but she seemed quite nonplused, even radiant.

For an unknown reason, in that light I suppose, something sparked in me. It wasn't like love at first sight; it was more like spring had popped. I think, when she glanced over at me, as if he didn't exist, by the look on her face, she felt the same.

A few days later, a friend called me.

"Do you want to dine at Maxim's tonight? Danielle will be there."

We dined together that evening and then adjourned to a boite to dance. We drank champagne and talked into the late hours, and then I took her home. As we stood at her door, she said, "Porfirio, I want you to know that this is serious."

Also for me, I replied.

That night I knew I would marry this woman. There would be my regular champagne and oysters, followed by passionate lovemaking, followed by a late omelet. A fork would ring out making contact with a plate and two pairs of lips would suck at each other, then on the rims of coffee mugs, then on the nape of a neck, and passion would rise again like a Phoenix.

I have never spoken to others about my lovers until these memoirs. I must say, aside from her striking facial features she had a lovely demure figure with skin as smooth as a used salt lick.

My diplomatic job was in Vichy, but my "job" was in Paris. I spent more time in the occupied zone than the free zone and everything seemed to be going okay until that day in December. Then the world really did change. It was December 7, 1941, and the Japanese attacked Pearl Harbor with a ferocity the world had never experienced.

It was self-evident that America would no longer stay out of the war.

I knew immediately that Santo Domingo would follow Washington, and I needed to take some precautions. My free traveling days were over. Paris was prohibited, and so I proposed to Danielle that we move.

✗

Rubirosa and the Dominican Legation moved to a building in Biarritz. The war terrified La Mome, so she fled with her husband to safer ground in Spain, and Rubi was left to play and travel freely between Vichy and Paris.

Later, in 1941, Rubi, unaccustomed to working more than an hour a week, nevertheless was in the Legation office in Paris, not in Vichy where the embassy was, when the French newspaper headlines read: *Germany Declares War on the United States.* World War II was officially underway.

As Rubi predicted, the Dominican Republic promptly joined the Allies, which technically made Rubi a representative of a "belligerent" country.

It was all symbolic for Trujillo. He sided with the Allies while his anticommunist policies gained favor in the United States.

Rubi couldn't return from Paris, so he called a German friend to pull some strings to get an authorization to travel back.

His friend thought it was possible and told him to come to his office immediately. However, when Rubi arrived, he was stunned to hear his friend questioning him reproachfully.

"What have you done?" he asked.

"Me? Nothing. What are you talking about?" Rubi replied.

Suddenly, when his friend and another German referred to him as *Mr.* Rubirosa, Rubi knew the tone of the conversation was going in a different direction than he'd expected.

"I am puzzled, Mr. Rubirosa. I wanted to help you, to intercede on your behalf, but we have discovered that you have a warrant out for your arrest. I have been ordered to detain you," the German said. Continuing: "However, since we are friends, I will not arrest you, but I will need your passport. Go to the German Embassy and ask for Mr. Von Kraft. He will explain this entire matter to you."

Once in the presence of Mr. Von Kraft, a man with a face as hard as a coffin nail, Rubi was summarily threatened and sternly lectured by the Gestapo-like embassy official.

"Your puny country dared to declare war on the great German Reich! Your President Trujillo insulted our Fuhrer in a speech. Do you realize you are in German jurisdiction? Consider yourself a prisoner!" Von Kraft yelled.

"You will be sent to the Claridge Hotel with a guard and be traded for the German Minister's life in Santo Domingo."

Unknown to Rubi, Trujillo had insulted Hitler when he declared his allegiance to the Allies. Rubi tried to reason with Von Kraft, telling him that there was a Dominican Minister in Berlin.

Bewilderment hung in the silence between them like a heavy curtain until Rubi turned to the solid footing of another topic.

"If anyone should be exchanged, it should be him, not me. I'm only a diplomat in Vichy. I happened to be in Paris only by accident."

"An accident?" the German inquired with a mean chuckle.

"Yes. An accident of love. I only came to Paris to see the one I love!"

The German laughed heartily and perhaps softened slightly, responding, "All right Mr. Rubirosa. If you promise me you won't try to escape, that you won't leave, I will let you remain under house arrest."

The following night, Rubi and Danielle visited L'aigion Restaurant, a dining spot that was as popular with German officers as with the French. A gypsy violinist serenaded the two lovers as several Gestapo officers were seated stoically nearby.

Rubi was drinking heavily, celebrating his "freedom" by tossing empty glasses over his shoulder, breaking them in the fireplace. He and Danielle were being loud and raucous, which incensed the Gestapo officers, particularly since she was French and he was a dark Latino.

Three weeks after my visit with Mr. Von Kraft, we went to the L'aigion I loved the gypsy violinist named Yoska Memeth. To us, he was simply Yoska.

I was well known in the nightlife, but Danielle was a "celebrity," a star. All of France sang about her. On the streets, people would recognize her and smile, or wave, or ask for an autograph. She always obliged with a smile and a toss of her hair, reaching into thin air, grasping, as if signaling for the fan to produce a pen and paper.

This night was no exception. There were throngs outside L'aigion, and they all smiled and yelled as Danielle and I came in. The orchestra was already in full swing and Yoska was going to great lengths to show off his talent.

At a nearby table, three German men were seated, dressed in civilian clothes, but they had that air of the Gestapo: stern, paranoid, and dangerous. Further away, at another table, was a high-ranking Wehrmact officer, maybe even a general.

Yoska came strolling towards us while playing his violin. By this time, I was drinking my third round of Russian vodka, Russian style, breaking the glasses in the fireplace by throwing them over my shoulder. I could see this was creating a tense atmosphere, like the first trickle of gravel that precipitates a landslide—but I didn't care.

One of the civilian Germans was the first to react. He was probably angry, not only with me, but because in 1942, a German victor could not be alone with a beautiful French woman.

Suddenly, the man stood up and threw his beer glass at me. This was a terrible insult and even knowing what the consequences might be, I could not help myself, and in my anger, I threw myself at him, striking the man in the face. He fell on the table, and then his two friends stood up and grabbed me. I was trapped. It was then that the General intervened, maybe to save my life. He separated us and then spoke to the two civilians in German, while speaking to me in French.

He told me, "I understand why you did this, but you don't know who you're dealing with. You must leave right away, right away."

The restaurant had grown silent. The public, the waiters, the musicians, everyone was petrified. Realizing our fate, I grabbed Danielle, and we ran to the door.

Whenever Yoska would relate that story, he would always say, "Mr. Rubirosa, it was God who put that German officer there because, otherwise, you would not be alive."

By strange coincidence, the next day, Von Kraft called Rubi to the Wilhelonstrasse building and he was told he would be sent to a city called Bad-Nauheim, home to a concentration camp for diplomats.

Once interred there, Rubi would meet delegates from around the world, all held prisoners. The entire Dominican Republic de Legation was there. During the long bus ride, Rubi became extremely depressed. His freedom was truly being taken away and he worried what would happen to Danielle.

It was the first time he could recall being depressed—bittersweet perhaps, pensive, but never depressed—over the loss of a woman, if only temporarily.

It was raining; an insidious fog began to feather its way over the wet streets as the bus wound its way toward the camp. A look of dim consternation creased Rubi's features. He pressed his hand to the window and wiped off the condensation, trying to get a bearing on where they were going. He was steeled for the worst: A vision of barbed wire stretched across used telephone poles acting as 30-foot fence posts.

There was a chance, he thought, that he'd never see Danielle again. Added to that, the prospects of sharing a threadbare bunk with strangers for an undetermined length of time, made him morose.

It was deemed a concentration camp, but it turned out, with Rubi's inevitable luck, to be a very social environment, with limited guards.

Men and women shared various rooms, not cells, and they would all wile away the time playing cards and listening to music. They even danced, which helped to keep Rubi occupied, but not happy. He saw little of the Dominican de Legation and instead was housed with strangers.

He said, "When one is in love, you can't simply wile away the time without living it."

Bad-Nauheim was a "thermal" city (natural hot springs). People came there from all over Europe to cure heart conditions. Unfortunately, the city had no such effect on my heart's condition.

While under house arrest, it was common for people (friends, lovers, and family) to send simple postcards, because

the guards would not then be ripping open our mail. I anxious-
ly awaited mail call every day. It was my only true diversion.

My newly minted friends were of no help. One of them told
me I was a disgrace to depression and the other said, "Don't
worry, you'll be back on your knees in no time."

In the small space of a postal card, I not only had to read
between the lines but between the words to discover love's
secrets, the song of the heart on lonely nights, or the com-
plaints of a faraway love. Nevertheless, these daily cards lifted my spirits, if only for a few hours. Until that little card
arrived each day, I dragged my bitter self along the corridors.
Then, when it arrived, I came to life.

After a few weeks, I began to befriend some of the people,
and I would jump up to the rooms on the first floor where my
new colleagues were and we'd get very drunk on white wine,
which we were able to acquire from one of the servants who
had a fondness for some of the young assistants of the
Dominican de Legation.

At some point, I began to think seriously about escaping.
Every time we turned on the radio, we heard the Japanese
broadcasts bragging about winning battles with the
Americans, and we heard the triumphant songs of the
Germans who were advancing into Russia.

I'm not a great strategist, however; I kept telling myself
that if London kept afloat and if the United States remained
okay, then the war really hadn't started. (The year was 1942.)
However, I did think that being incarcerated was going to last
awhile, and the separation from Danielle was unbearable. I
hadn't felt this lost since the invention of misery.

After five months of incarceration, Rubi was set
free. Recognizing Danielle as the best-known movie star in
France, and Rubi's "girlfriend," it was decided that an
exchange would be made with other Latin American diplomats.

It was rumored that Danielle was a sympathizer. At the time, the Nazis wanted French actors to visit studios in Berlin and Munich, perhaps to make propaganda films, so the Germans decided the de Legation would be incomplete without her and she was invited, along with Rubi, to live in a hotel for three months in Berlin.

Rubi had been saved by a woman, which would set a pattern for the rest of his life. He had been beyond anguish—"a strip mining of the soul," as he put it—but others felt he deserved it.

We were no longer in a state of anxiety. The abundance viewed through the windows of shops, the shining electric lights without "blackout," without blue windows, without opaque light bulbs.

People everywhere with happy faces; it was infectious. I spent my first two or three days without having had the impression of walking on air. It was as if I'd been floating around, confused, under a spell.

Danielle had to go to Vichy but we spoke over the phone, we spoke over the borders, over the walls that had turned Europe into a dungeon, over the army of soldiers and police; we spoke of our love for one another.

We got married as soon as I arrived in Vichy, without any publicity, and spent our honeymoon in Portugal where Danielle was received as a queen; they even organized a special bullfight in her honor. There was a full orchestra in the stands and as we took our seats, everyone in the stadium rose to applaud, with the notable exception of the German Ambassador.

The following day, the students at the University of Santarem threw their capes at her feet and applauded and through it all, Danielle remained very modest.

Upon their return to Vichy, the two retired temporarily to

Danielle's property in Ile de France. However, the tranquility didn't last long.

One morning in November of 1942, the Germans erupted into Vichy and it became increasingly difficult, if not impossible, for Rubi to correspond with Santo Domingo. The atmosphere became unbearable and so Rubi decided to put some distance between the Germans, himself, and his new bride.

They packed quickly, taking only the necessities, much of it in two leather bags and backpacks. Rubi was at his adventuresome best, taking charge, acting decisively, and relishing what their next move might be.

Though Danielle was a petite woman, she also moved with an air of abandon. She padded about the house looking determined and unafraid—a barefoot soldier being led into psychological battle by invisible generals.

Soon the German Gestapo would be chasing Rubi.

They rented a chalet in Megeve, mainly because Rubi could ski there (it was close to Switzerland); he also had many friends living there. It, too, was occupied, but by the Italians, not the Germans, so the atmosphere was completely different, not as harsh.

Shortly after they arrived, Rubi and Danielle found themselves living in a guarded residence. The Dominican Republic had broken off relations with the Vichy government and Rubi had little status.

However, he obtained permission to stay in their Megevian chalet with the condition that he present himself every morning to the gendarmerie.

That month, sympathy for the resistance began to grow and a collection of money for the maquis (resistance) was organized. Rubi participated and when the Italian captain found out, he summoned him.

"Mr. Rubirosa. I heard that you are participating in the collection for the maquis. If you continue to play this little game, it could cost you…." He stopped there. "A word to the wise is sufficient."

Rubi didn't respond, but nodded his head.

He may have indicated with a nod that he understood, but Rubi pressed on, even to the point that he was dictating operations to the growing number of resistance supporters as the townspeople continued to rally.

The Germans were not happy. There was a Gestapo center representative in Megeve and another in Austria run by a man known simply as Otto, a ferocious looking goliath nearly six feet five inches tall with a bald head as large as a pumpkin. A thick blonde mustache draped down the sides of his mouth past his chin.

He was a formidable nemesis who was an excellent skier, was as familiar with the mountains as a pack of wolves, and spoke French as well as several other languages. He had attacked the maquis at their own game and had made many successful hits on their ranks.

One afternoon, a resistance group met at Rubi's home, telling him they wanted to attack Otto when he left his house in Megeve, but Rubi intervened, warning them that there would be reprisals for everyone. "Instead," he told them, "ambush him on the road. He is cunning and dangerous, so make sure you take several men and at least one marksman."

The maquis leaders left and during the next few days, they tried to ambush Otto on the road, to no avail. Eventually, two men came down from the mountain. These were the type of men who didn't care about reprisals. On the contrary, reprisals just incited the villagers to hate, which led more of them to join the maquis.

The two men went straight to Otto's house, confronted him at his own front door, and immediately shot him in both eyes.

The echo of the shots had barely subsided when all the men in Megeve fled to hide in the mountains. I alone stayed, not out of bravery, but because as a Dominican diplomat, I wasn't allowed to leave.

However, something curious happened—the Germans didn't act immediately. Several weeks passed and still nothing. Slowly, everyone began returning to the town, thinking the danger was over. Naturally, that is when the trucks filled with German soldiers began arriving, first blocking the entrances and exits of the town.

There is no honor in entering the food chain, so we stayed silent as hoards of jack-booted soldiers in spiked helmets jumped off the backs of flatbed trucks, bayonets fixed on their rifles. Danielle said she felt as if a swarm of black butterflies were fluttering in her stomach, though, as always she remained stoic.

Orders were shouted as several higher ranking enlisted men jabbed and pointed for the people to stand in various lines.

The Jewish villagers were the first to go. We found out later, they had been taken to Montluc, the prison in Lyon, and from there, they were deported to God knows where.

Both the Italians and the Germans now occupied us.

One day, I ran into Otto's wife in town. She motioned to me with a turn of her head. I understood and followed her silently, playing dumb. When we were alone, she told me, "Be careful,

Rubi. Right before he died, my husband told me that the Gestapo from Chamonix was convinced that you are part of the intelligence service. You are being watched closely. They have you on a short leash. One day they will pull in the reins and you'll be trapped. You must leave Megeve immediately."

Her warning saved my life. The next day, I told my skiing friend, Jean Pierre, about the problem and that I had to escape Megeve. I told him I would need accomplices and help. He solved my transportation problem by providing me a car that one of his friends would drive. His name was Ralph and he happened to be a racecar driver.

What a great friend Pierre was. Not only did he obtain a car and expert driver, but he prepared a hiding place for me and Danielle in Paris and faked documents for us under the names of Peter Richard and Georgette Allais. He even procured a costume for Danielle. Her document photos were taken of her with an enormous pair of glasses and wearing a silly hat.

The best hiding place in Paris was on the Avenue Commandant Charcot, in Neuilly. In reality, it was more like a revolving door where the members of the alambrada (those on the run) ended up, armed to the teeth, which worried Danielle constantly.

Ralph, the driver, was there as was Jean Wimille and Pierre Legonie. The conversations were always about helping others, certain operations, and lots of sabotage.

One day, returning to our apartment, the manager informed me that the German police had come to look for me. Danielle and I were obviously not happy about this outcome.

Danielle said, "If we stay here, then something bad is going to happen to us. I have a little farm in Ile-de-France in Septuil. It's about 60 kilometers from Paris. We would be much safer there."

So, that's where we went to live during what turned out to be the last few months of the occupation.

I turned into, of all things, a farmer. I bought a cow and learned how to milk it so we could have milk and butter. We bought two pigs for ham, and six sheep for leg of lamb.

Occasionally, friends would come over, share cognac, and leave weapons with us for safekeeping.

One afternoon as I was attending to the cow, the grand-daughter of one of the officials of Courgent arrived, out of breath.

"Sir," she said, "there are militiamen at my father's house; people in uniforms with guns. They are looking for the house of Danielle Darrieux. Father had me leave the garden and come directly to warn you."

I knew immediately what it was about. A few days earlier, a perfectly repugnant article had been published in a local newspaper. I had been denounced as a servant of Judeo-Marxist plutocrats. The article also noted that I was living with Danielle and the brave, anonymous author of the publication wondered why I wasn't behind bars.

I called Danielle and we jumped on our bicycles, pedaling up the road that led to a small hill covered with trees, which was behind a house. From there, we could spy on the arriving trucks full of soldiers in navy blue uniforms, the militiamen. We could clearly see Danielle's house and then the servant coming out. I had given her instructions. After a few moments of conversation, they left.

I didn't know that I could completely trust our servant, so Danielle and I spent the next few days hiding in a friend's barn.

After that, with the exception of an occasional British bomber being hit by German flack, one landing only 400 yards from our house, things became quieter. However, we got word that every day the Germans were retreating further and further north from Normandy, and that the Allies had landed in force.

Then, one afternoon, while in Nantes, we met our first

American. It was in a café. There was a group of young men visiting who were talking loudly. One of them pointed at Danielle.

"Danielle Darrieux," he said with an accent, dragging the "eux" out. He was an American pilot and we got to know each other quickly. They were all dying for some fresh food and we were longing for American products, so we bartered canned food for fresh vegetables and celebrated our first night of liberation. The Allies (Americans) had indeed arrived and the war would soon be over.

Later, when Paris was free, the couple returned to the capital. The celebrating was short-lived, however. Once again, there would be the deafening sounds of gunfire and explosions.

The war was "officially" over in August of 1944, but that didn't silence the gunfire. One early September evening, Danielle and I had been invited to a party in Paris. Our friends, Bill Hearst and Vassilopoulos, a Greek diplomat, who was accompanied by his wife, Edmee, joined us.

At two in the morning, it was very still outside as we all climbed into Vassilopoulos' car for the ride home to Neuilly. We took the Boulevard Malsheres. I sat in the back in between Danielle and a young Swiss man, a friend of Vassilopoulos'.

As we motored slowly and quietly down the boulevard, I heard a familiar sound and then Danielle said, "Hey, that was a shot." Vassilopoulos slowed the car nearly to a halt and then all hell broke loose with the rat-a-tatta-tat of machine guns—several of them, I guessed.

Edmee screamed like a banshee. The gunfire was coming from behind us and she'd been hit, but I didn't realize it at that moment. It all happened in the time it takes to blink. Bullets continued to shatter the back window and as Danielle and I instinctively bent over, I felt searing pain shoot through my back. My God, I thought, what in the hell is going on?

A hundred thoughts seemed to race through my mind simultaneously. Who were these people? Why were they shooting at us? Is Danielle okay? Am I okay?

I felt as if I'd been stabbed with a red-hot fire poker. Nevertheless, I peeked up at Edmee, who was bleeding profusely and still screaming. Vassilopoulos seemed all right and Danielle was doubled up next to me, trembling, but was not hit.

Vassilopoulos cradled his wife in his arms and kept repeating, "Don't die, Edmee. Don't die." No more than 20 seconds had passed. Looking back, it felt like an hour, and then it was silent again.

The pain in my back was becoming worse. I opened my collar as my face and palms began to sweat profusely and I became nauseous. Danielle sat up and put her arm around me, asking if I was okay. I didn't want to alarm her, so I just said, I'm not feeling well.

Amidst all the confusion, the Swiss man jumped out of the car unharmed and began to shout deliriously, "What about people's rights? What about civilization and liberty? Is it possible that people can still be murdered in the streets of Paris, even though the war is over?" He kept shouting and rambling.

I turned to Danielle and said: Leave him. There is nothing to be gained by shouting. Take us to the hospital.

She immediately sprang into action. "Are you all right? Are you hurt?" she asked.

Yes, I answered. But I think I'm wounded (yet I couldn't see any blood).

By this time, I could hardly breathe. I felt like something unexplainable was leaving me, no doubt it was my life, or what little soul I had. However, at that same instant, I felt a strange power surge, a jump in energy.

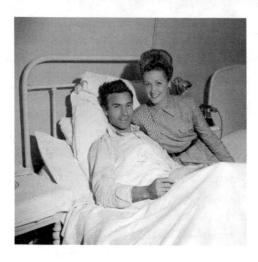

Just the first of many times Rubi would cheat death (with Danielle in a Paris hospital)

Knowing the area as I did, I yelled to Vassilopoulos to take us to Marmottan, the emergency hospital, a distant memory from my childhood, a neighborhood nearby that I knew well.

Giving him directions, I pointed and said: Turn left here, now right. A few more blocks. In a few moments, we arrived at the large stainless steel swinging doors of the emergency room. Edmee was slumped over, motionless in the front seat.

Orderlies surrounded the car and opened all the doors. First, they took Edmee out on a stretcher. Next, I tried to swing my legs out and stand up, but they gave out. Another orderly brought out a wheelchair and two of them lifted me into it—still no sight of blood, but a horrible stabbing pain throbbed in my right lower back, near my kidney.

I was dropped off in a room filled with wounded soldiers. Danielle stood by my side holding my hand. I felt so bad for her. She was obviously scared to death, but was trying hard not to show her emotions.

I knew this hospital. It was the nearest, but it wasn't the best. Half the doctors were good, the other half were nearly inept. I told Danielle to call Dr. Frank Bretano, one of the great surgeons in Paris, who'd operated on me when I'd had appendicitis.

When she found his number and he answered (at 3 a.m.) she shouted into the phone as if it were his fault we were all here.

"Doctor, Rubi must have been shot several times—in the kidneys, I think, but there is very little blood on his shirt," she told him.

"Can he move his legs?"

"I don't know. I suppose so. He can't walk."

Danielle hung up the phone and said, "He isn't coming. He says it's better for the doctors here to see to you. Some surgeon," she added sarcastically.

My wound was so serious that even a famous surgeon refused the case, afraid he might lose such a "famous" patient. Apparently, whatever my "celebrity," it wasn't enough to save my life.

By now, Edmee was already in the operating room. I didn't know what to do. There was just Danielle and me sitting, waiting in a room full of moaning and groaning wounded GIs. I wondered how many of them had far more serious wounds than me.

As the pain mounted, and time seemed to hold in suspension, I lit up a cigarette to calm myself. Just then a nurse came in and asked, "What are you doing here?"

I think I have a bullet in my back, I answered.

"And you're not saying anything?" she said. "I'm going to find a doctor." And, with that, she disappeared. Good idea, I thought.

When the doctor arrived, he pushed me forward in the wheelchair and looked at my back.

"Take this man to surgery immediately," he yelled in a panicked voice, which did not give me a great deal of confidence.

"Prepare the anesthesia," he shouted as he left the room.

Riding down the long gray hallways on a gurney, I looked up at a beautiful nurse and asked: Do you think I'll live?

"Yes, Cherie. Not to worry," she said.

Within seconds of them putting the mask over my face, I was out. I don't even remember nodding off.

I didn't wake up until late the next day. They told me the operation lasted nearly three hours. The day after that I was transferred to a regular hospital in Neuilly. Danielle never left my side over the next few days, as I lay in a pool of continuous sweat, delirious, hallucinating. I didn't know it, of course, but I was fighting off a serious infection.

Edmee wound up in the room next to me. Her buttock wound had not been life threatening. I had a hole in my back the size of a teacup. When the intern finally came into the room and I asked him, half awake, if he thought I'd live, he said calmly, "If within five days, there is no longer any infection, you will live. If not, there probably won't be anything we can do."

As simple as that. Five days. If you're still alive, you'll probably live.

All I could think of was the fortuneteller Frau Ackerman that I'd visited in Berlin in 1936, nearly eight years before. She'd told me that within two years, I would be divorced and within eight, I would be in a serious accident involving firearms. I also remembered vividly that she said I would miraculously recover.

She'd been right on all counts.

Several weeks later, the bandits had been identified and arrested—turned out they weren't gangsters or leftover German subversives—young men who were playing war, trying to make a belated statement of some sort, however misguided and dangerous.

Rubi ended up staying at the clinic for a month before they let him go home. He'd taken three bullets near his right kidney and it was a miracle he lived.

Media reports and conjecture offered several other, more diabolical answers for the attack. Alternately, it was Danielle's ex-husband who perpetrated the attack, or they were Germans still angry with Rubi for secreting Jews out of Germany during the war. Nothing was ever proven.

Years later, the story evolved and morphed into one of heroism on Rubi's part. It was reported that immediately upon hearing the initial gunfire, Rubi plunged to his left and covered Danielle with his body to protect her and in so doing, was shot himself.

✗

By the time Rubi went home to Paris, a provisional government had been installed with Charles de Gaulle as president. Rubi thought he was going to be reassigned, but it was decided that any diplomats who had been in Vichy wouldn't be assigned to Paris, no matter where they came from.

After that incident, Rubi and Danielle moved to Septuil, about 30 miles west of Paris where they lived for the next three years. Rubi continued his role as a gentleman farmer of sorts and shortly thereafter, Danielle went back to making movies. As a result, they moved to Rome where they stayed in a hotel.

For a long time, Rubi was faithful. Their life together was passionate and blissful. Danielle was the woman that Rubi loved most. However, that did not keep him from adding more adventures to his legend.

At a party given by the international playboy Prince Aly Khan on the Riviera that year, an Argentine millionairess was flirting with Rubi at a Casino table. Someone informed her husband and he challenged Rubi to a duel. Fortunately, Prince Aly's intervention prevented the incident from escalating into a tragedy.

It seemed that five years was Rubi's limit. Had he and Danielle remained in Paris, things might have been different. However, Danielle was filled with disillusionment and homesickness for France. Their marriage was about to take a turn for the worse.

Like an extraordinary performance, the applause eventually gave way to the clatter of falling scenery and the closing of curtains.

One day, while in Rome, a writer from *Harpers Bazaar* magazine came to their hotel room to interview Danielle. The writer was a woman named Doris Duke, who was also the heiress to the $100 million American Tobacco fortune.

Welcome to the high life
Rubi and Doris at El Morocco

The ambition of most men is to make money. Mine is to spend it.

– Porfirio Rubirosa

Doris Duke's $100-million fortune in those days would be worth closer to a few billion in today's dollars. Her father was James B. Duke, tobacco tycoon, namesake of Duke University and one of the richest men in the country.

Doris inherited her father's fortune when she was just 13. From nearly that point on, she always made headlines. She had been a war correspondent, then later, the owner of an Italian newspaper, *Rome-American Daily*. Much later, in 1988, at the age of 76, she continued to make headlines by posting bail for the former Philippine First Lady, Imelda Marcos.

According to a biography, *The Richest Girl in the World*, by Stephanie Mansfield, "The headlines don't even begin to tell one of the most compelling and fascinating stories of our time. A maverick from an early age, the somewhat attractive and very eccentric heiress thumbed her nose at society, all the while forging an incredible life as a renegade with an appetite for adventure, a weakness for pleasure, and a penchant for privacy."

During the war, she'd been employed with the OSS (the fore-runner to today's CIA). When the war was over, she was terminated and needed a reason to stay in Europe. While in Rome, she met three former *Stars and Stripes* (Armed Forces newspaper) journalists who were also reluctant to go home. Doris, always the entrepreneurial one, persuaded the three to join her in launching an English language tabloid, *The Rome Daily American.* Doris named herself the "society editor."

It wasn't long, though, before the relationship soured and she returned to Paris where she wrote dispatches and columns for the INS bureau (Inter-national News Service).

It was 1946 when Rubi and Doris met in the hotel where he and Danielle were staying.

Rubi was immediately smitten with Duke's certain "American *'je ne sais quoi'*." He saw her as lively and exciting, in a way that only American women can be and, of course, she was bright and opinionated, which was also appealing to him, if only for the challenge.

Within months, he was completely under her spell. He was 37; she was 30.

According to Rubi's polo pal, Gerard Bonnet, Duke sent Rubi a telegram following their first encounter, which read: "When you're finished with Danielle, give me a call and I will come."

Shortly thereafter, she wrote again: "Arriving immediately."

The three of us had breakfast that next day. Doris appeared to be jovial and full of life. I knew that she owned the Rome Daily American, and that her father was the president of the American Tobacco Company, but little else. It never occurred to me at the time that I might become captivated with her in just a few months. I felt that Danielle and I were happy. However, looking back years later at this writing, I realize she was quite unhappy with me.

It wasn't long after I met Doris, however, that Danielle wanted a separation. Danielle had, among other things, become a great comedic actress, and was being offered everything she could ever have dreamed of by all sorts of Hollywood producers. They all wanted to "discover" her and bring her to California.

Little by little, I had to force myself to divide my time between Rome and Paris, and to live two lives. Though there were less than 1,000 kilometers between us, something more than absence was transpiring. It is sad to see your other half, your echo, slip away from you. I still loved her.

Doris Duke
Paid $1,000,000 for Rubi

In the end, we had one final sad conversation. She was angered when I wouldn't come to Morocco where she was filming and later, when we joined again in Paris, she said I was useless. I realized in that heartrending final dialogue just how lonely I'd made her feel, how little respect I'd really given her. I think—no, I'm sure—that was the first time my heart had been broken, and I was to blame.

I was made even sadder by the fact that she wasn't angry with me, she had simply given up. The entire encounter astounded me, and it was the first time I could remember feeling that I'd really screwed up and lost a very, very good thing.

Once it goes, it's gone. There is no snatching back the exhilaration or the comforts of sharing souls; like a champagne bottle dropped on the sidewalk, there is no way to glue a love back together, and there is no mending of the heartache, other than time.

Once I felt that ache, that emptiness, I felt even worse, knowing exactly what she was feeling. I don't know which was worse.

X

Regardless of his melancholy, through the passage of time, Rubi eventually recovered and was thriving on the nightlife once again. This time, however, he was drinking with abandon and even began to experiment with morphine and his health degraded. If only temporarily, he had become so popular that he could not go unnoticed in the clubs.

He was soon drowning his sorrows not only with drugs and alcohol, but a succession of affairs. When it was rumored he was at a certain hotel, within hours, throngs of women would assemble outside longing for even a glimpse of the famous Rubirosa.

Eventually, Doris Duke entered Rubi's life again: elegant, happy, enchanting—ready to reinvigorate the forlorn lover. Soon, Rubi was feeling alive again. His substance abuse subsided and he quickly returned to form.

Very early on, Doris had decided to marry Rubi, and would obviously get no resistance from him, yet she didn't realize that at the time. If necessary, she would buy him the way she bought a Rembrandt. She would deal shrewdly, as she did in all her business transactions, until she got what she wanted at the lowest possible price.

It is rumored that Doris offered Rubi a cool million dollars to divorce Danielle and alternately, that she paid Danielle the million. She may have paid them both, or Doris might not have precipitated Rubi and Danielle's breakup at all, depending upon what you read.

According to *Too Rich: The Family Secrets of Doris Duke* by Pony Duke and Jason Thomas, "Instead of interviewing the superstar, Doris negotiated with Danielle for the purchase of her husband.

"The exact words that were exchanged by the two women (as Rubi sat nearby on a Louis XV settee in silence) have remained a secret, but Doris proved that she had indeed inherited Buck Duke's ability to negotiate for what she wanted.

"Doris pointed out that Rubi would probably leave Danielle eventually, anyway. She also called attention to the fact that the once-adored actress was now a pariah in France and fans would no longer be willing to pay their francs to be entertained by a traitor. Her career ruined, she should consider liquidating some of her more expensive assets—of which, Rubi was the most expensive. The two sophisticated women began to negotiate.

"Danielle suggested that $5 million seemed fair. Without taking a breath, Doris offered $1 million, not a penny more. She pointed out that $1 million in American dollars was worth a lot of francs in the ravaged postwar French economy.

"All French women are very pragmatic when it comes to matters of money and Danielle was no exception. She took the million. Doris would have paid more and she was so pleased with the deal that she gave Rubirosa an additional $500,000 as a signing bonus, which it is reported, he later used to buy a coffee plantation."

According to Danielle, "Since Rubi had no intention of changing, there was no choice but to get a divorce. I had waited long to tell him these things, until I was sure of myself, sure that I could live without him, and sure that I wouldn't be tempted to rush back to his side.

"Now, I can say farewell."

Isn't it odd? Sometimes a man can't win. If he runs after money, he's money-mad; if he keeps it, he's a capitalist; if he spends it, he's a playboy; if he doesn't get it, he's a ne'er-do-well; if he doesn't try to get it, he lacks ambition. If he gets it without working for it, he's a parasite; and if he accumulates it after a lifetime of hard work, people call him a fool who never got anything out of life.

Doris found Rubi's constant fawning unusual but immensely charming and she showered him with gifts in return.

Rubi was willing to earn his keep so besides the sex, he always tried to match her generosity by giving her gifts that were as tasteful and carefully selected as the presents she gave him.

The relationship between these two kindred souls would eventually cause headlines even Doris had never dreamed possible. The State Department even became involved when they stated they were appalled at Doris' choice of companions. They refused to allow her to stay in Europe and threatened to cancel her passport. They felt she was harming American prestige by being seen with unsavory characters—chiefly, Porfirio Rubirosa.

Based on FBI documents, it is more likely that the State Department feared that Rubi would have unfettered access to Duke's war chest.

Duke was the most powerful woman in America and she controlled huge amounts of power energy, chiefly gas, oil, and electricity. Her father's company provided much of the electric energy for vast areas of the Southern U.S., an area that coincidentally contained some of the largest military installations in the country, which just made the State Department that much more nervous. She owned much of

Texaco with interests in aluminum (the basis for the growing aircraft industry).

The State Department feared that if Duke married Rubi and died, Rubi would inherit the empire, which would then ostensibly come under the control of the Dominican Republic.

The OSS was horrified. The White House even debated what to do in the few hours before the wedding. Some OSS officials seriously considered killing Rubirosa.

An FBI memo we obtained states: "The reported marriage of Porfirio Rubirosa to heiress Doris Duke, on September 1, 1947. It had been disclosed previously in Paris that Rubirosa had been appointed Dominican Ambassador to Argentina.

"Concerning the marriage of Doris Duke to Rubirosa, it was indicated that Rubirosa was honorary Charge d' Affairs of the Dominican Republic, although he was not recognized by the French because he had once been acceptable to the Vichy Regime."

This was just the beginning of the FBIs interest in the heiress and the playboy diplomat.

Prior to the wedding, Rubi was in great spirits, joking with friends and fawning over Doris until two men in dark suits, wearing stern expressions, showed up. One of them presented a large manila envelope to Rubi and asked him to sit down.

The two large men stood behind Rubi with their arms folded over their chests and glowered down on him, each with a large bulge on the side of his suit jacket. They were from Duke's "law firm."

While all about him were reveling in the moment, drinking champagne, and Doris was strategically standing across the room, Rubi opened the envelope and read the cover sheet.

He seemed to be in a state of suspended animation as he

read the document entitled: *Prenuptial Agreement between Doris Duke and Porfirio Rubiroso*. (It was actually the diplomatic corps that suggested the agreement. After a meeting with these officials, Doris relented and told them to take care of the problem without harming Rubi or any of his five precious appendages.)

At first, he didn't understand the implications and then he proceeded to get drunk enough to finally sign it before evening's end. It was rumored that the OSS had drugged him.

At just over six feet, the bride was three inches taller than Rubi. She wore a Dior suit to the wedding with a matching green velvet hat. Rubi wore a simple smoking jacket with a pair of pinstriped pants. However, the entire scene and prenuptial matter unnerved him greatly, so he chain-smoked throughout the entire ceremony.

The guests were stunned, and a Frenchman observed that Rubi was rude and had no respect for the source of his pending wealth.

Immediately after the ceremony, Rubi began to drink and did not stop until he passed out on a settee. A few of the bewildered guests tried to revive him, to no avail.

The couple honeymooned in the Alps and afterward established residence in Paris. Duke purchased a three-story 17th century mansion on the left bank of the Seine, paying $100,000 for the property.

The mansion was spectacular and had been owned by a princess. A well-known decorator was hired to complement Duke's own design talents and soon, the palatial home was filled with heirlooms, paintings, and Louis XV and XVI pieces.

Originally, the top floor was designed as servant's quarters, but Rubi gutted it and built a custom boxing ring and a full bar. He also did his own decorating in the "gym/bar," hanging dozens of pictures of himself and friends on polo ponies, along with his medals and various trophies from polo matches.

It is said that many mornings around 4:00 a.m., when Rubi

would return from another round of revelry in the cabarets, a trio of guitarists from the Calvados nightclub would follow him home and set up their instruments inside the ring, and the party would continue. Rubi's butler would serve beer, scotch, and tortilla omelets to everyone.

A team of servants tended to the couple's every whim and need. Two Spanish maids, who wore raw silk uniforms, continuously dusted the paintings and glossy Louis furniture, and a chef was on call 24-hours a day to prepare Rubi's favorite dishes. A chauffeur was always on hand as well, to drive Duke's many American luxury cars and to polish the growing fleet of Rubi's Italian racing cars that Doris had purchased for him.

The couple also loved to entertain and there was a constant flow of celebrities, royalty, and the just plain famous. Among the visitors were Joe and Rose Kennedy, the Queen of Yugoslavia, Baron Elie Rothschild, and many other dignitaries.

In an article by writer Diogenes Reyna, he had this to say:

"In a biography published by a prestigious Latin American magazine, I read about Doris Duke's life.

"When she touched on the subject of one of her husbands (Rubi), she defined him as 'a man who got what he wanted.'

"'The time we were together made me very happy. I liked his company. He was a very bold man for his time with an extraordinary vision of the future. This definition from one of his wives has made me understand Porfirio better. He is an advanced man for his time. He demonstrated it in the way he carried himself, and in the way he dressed.

"'He was the first international jetsetter to wear 'blue jeans' or 'workers,' as they used to call them. He wore them with a jacket and no tie, and he was the first one to be seen in casual shoes (loafers) without socks.'"

Theirs seemed the idealic marriage, filled with gaiety and frivolity. Neither partner seemed to have a care in the world, but with Rubi's wandering spirit always a potential contention, the next prettier face was never far away.

One evening, when the Dominican Ambassador—who was also an MD—came to Paris, he visited the Rubirosas. When he arrived and inquired about Doris' whereabouts, Rubi told him that Doris was in bed with a high fever. The doctor went upstairs immediately and determined she had the flu. He gave Rubi a prescription to fill and asked him to find an open drugstore, which proved to be a difficult task at 5:30 in the morning.

As Rubi wandered the streets in search of the medicine, he passed an underground bar called Tabou. The lure was too strong for Rubi, who felt like having a scotch. One drink led to another and soon a day and evening had passed. Rubi returned home the following morning, having left his sick wife home in bed for an entire day and night.

On another occasion, Doris asked Rubi to buy her some cigarettes and on his way, he ran into an old friend who persuaded Rubi to join him for a drink. Three days later, Doris was still waiting for her cigarettes—the tobacco queen was being deprived of tobacco.

Back home, Trujillo, once again the Rubi fan, delighted in the news that Rubi had landed such a fine catch as Duke. His admiration for Rubi's conquest, adventures, and exploits convinced him it would be in his best interests to appoint Rubi to an ambassadorship somewhere that would provide political and economic connections for the President.

Soon, Rubi had received a letter from Trujillo offering him a post anywhere he chose in South America. Rubi, still enamored of Paris, and not thrilled with the prospect of moving, nevertheless chose Argentina—probably for that country's love of polo more than anything else.

I had always been excited about riding and playing, especially because I learned it at a time when the techniques were taking a new turn.

This is one of the oldest sports in the world. The Persians played it before Christ. In Isaphan (in Persia) near the palace, there is a great square, which used to be polo grounds. Sultans watched the game from their balconies, as it was part of the magnificence of Darius' empire. Polo, from the Tibetan word "pallu-balle," was played at the frontier of India and Persia. That is where the British soldiers discovered it and then brought it back to Europe.

Gradually, the game was gaining more virility. Players started to play faster, which meant more violence.

For a long time, the horse the player rode was small. However, due to the new trends, it was replaced with a thoroughbred, which was a stronger, faster animal.

A world champion polo player, Rubi was an ambassador for the sport.

Unexpectedly, it began to lose fans in Biarritz. To tell the truth, the audience that frequented these grounds never reached a thousand people. What a shame! Polo is a spectacular and popular game and Argentineans know that.

If there are a couple dozen players in Paris, there are no less than 4,000 in Argentina. And, if there are 200 spectators in Paris, it is no wonder that by the end of the "first open," some 20,000 cheering fans attended the game in Argentina.

Rubi traveled to Argentina alone. Doris was beset with family and more State Department problems. Her family did not approve of her moving to South America with the "scandalous" Dominican, nor did they feel she would be safe there.

Porfirio Rubirosa shakes hands with President Juan D. Peron of Argentina in Bueno Aires prior to presenting his credentials to Peron as ambassador from the Dominican Republic.

The State Department had been relentless in the intolerance for her reproachable actions in foreign nations, but there really was little they could do; they never ceased to badger her.

Finally, in December of 1947, Doris flew to Buenos Aires to join Rubi. She had chartered a second plane to bring all their Louis furniture and servants.

The couple was an immediate hit on the Argentine social circuit and were warmly welcomed. Rubi was given the nickname "The Black Boxer" in one newspaper headline.

The couple began to receive invitations immediately. One day they were attending a function with pink champagne and the next, they were visiting places of special interest as tourists, or being honored at private receptions. They were also given a luxurious five-room apartment.

Rubi continued to enjoy his new wealth and even began donating money to charities, most notably, Eva Peron's pet projects. Evita was grateful, saying it was the first time a diplomat had shown any interest in her charities. A rival ambassador put it differently: "It is the first time in recorded history that a pimp ever gave money to a harlot."

Another version of this story painted a different picture. It was reported by a tabloid that while Eva was showing him around, Rubi offended her by constantly looking at his watch. He realized later that he'd been rude and to smooth relations, he donated money to her charity.

Juan Peron was a center-right dictator in the mold of a Franco. Trujillo's interest was in finding out what that meant for the Dominican Republic and he knew Rubi would find out, even if it meant sleeping with Eva, which it is reported he did in short order.

Eva Peron
A different type of
diplomacy

Her opening line when they met was: "I believe you divorce rather frequently, Your Excellency," to which he replied, "When quarrels are frequent, when life together is a trial rather than a pleasure, it is better to separate."

With the exception of the backlash from the diplomatic corps over Rubi's attention to Eva, life in Argentina was wonderful, at least for Rubi. Doris had just surprised him with the gift of an airplane—a restored World War II, B-25 Bomber, which he loved. What pilot wouldn't?

Rubi promptly used it to fly to Paris for a polo match. He had decided to take his valet with him and he asked him to obtain a French visa, but it was discovered that the valet had only a Russian passport so his visa was denied. Rubi appealed to the Brazilian Ambassador for help, asking that since Trujillo had declared hostilities to the Communists, absolute discretion was required.

✗

Within a few days, the visa was granted and the two flew to Rio de Janeiro where the Bomber was stationed. Trips to Rio de Janeiro became a regular diversion for Rubi. On one occasion, while on one of these trips, he threw a party for about 50 people, including friends and at least two former lovers. Later in that evening, he locked himself and a friend into one of the bathrooms for the duration of the evening. Rumor has it that it was Danielle.

For Doris, it was another story. She hated Latin America: the heat and humidity and the poverty. Most of all, she hated Rubi's philandering, so it wasn't long before she was fed up with the entire scene. She adored him and wanted to keep her property, but he wasn't about to change, and he told her so, sighting she'd always known what he was like. Nothing had changed.

Was it generosity then, or spite, that caused the two to begin giving away each other's possessions? Through all the free-spending, both seemed to enjoy giving away extravagant presents. Doris would complain whenever Rubi awarded his best polo players with Doris' cars, and he would get angry when she would give her musicians Rubi's silk suits and shirts.

The two continued to fight and Rubi continued to play the field, when one day, he received a summons from Trujillo to return to Santo Domingo. Rubi felt a surge of fear for his life. Knowing he would have to return, he decided to take Doris with him as an insurance policy. Surely, the president would not harm him in the presence of such a well-known and wealthy American woman, he surmised. In fact, the dictator did treat them very well, giving a splendid banquet in their honor and inviting them to his country estate for a picnic.

Had Rubi stopped in Argentina before returning to Santo Domingo, he would have read the telegram informing him of his suspension as ambassador. Instead, he received the news from the source.

Apparently, the final straw for Trujillo came after one of Rubi's final Argentine trysts led to an international scandal. A wealthy, married socialite became obsessed with him and even later followed him to Paris. When she caught up with him in Paris, he fled to Rome.

Doris was fed up with Rubi. She fled to Hawaii and Rubi went to Rome with several suitcases filled with cash.

Shortly after arriving, Rubi, as usual, made a beeline to one of his favorite nightspots and while dancing with a young beauty, was stunned to look across the bar to see his ex-wife, Flor, seated with another woman.

Though reports are sketchy, the two were seen for the next few weeks frequenting various nightspots, and it didn't take long for word to get back to Doris who was in Hawaii. She immediately left, arriving in New York on July 2, 1948. From there, she boarded an ocean liner, telling reporters she was "ill and terribly upset."

She had wired Rubi from New York because when she arrived in Cherbourg, France, on the 28th, he was there to meet her. Rubi quickly "dumped" Flor as he and Doris reunited. Doris even sent for her three German shepherds, who were immediately flown to Paris.

However, the cozy state of affairs didn't last long. According to Rubi, "She got this craze for jazz music all of a

sudden. All day she practiced the piano and she got this professor, a girl, to teach her. She wanted to study so much, she
asked the girl to move into the house with us and I didn't like
that, so there were fights."

The two also fought over money. It frustrated Rubi that he
did not have any true control over his own finances. He even
tried to interest her in buying a fleet of cargo ships, but her
attorney balked at that idea, saying he wanted them so he
could transport illegal arms from one Latin-American republic to another.

Later that same month, Rubi flew to New York in his
$50,000 B-25 and had to crash-land it in a swamp in New
Jersey. The plane was eventually repaired.

Upon returning and indulging immediately in a night of
celebrating, he went home to find Doris unconscious. She had
cut her wrists and there was blood all over the room.

She was splayed out absurdly across the white down com-
forter, rivulets of blood tracing down from her arms across the
satin and onto the floor.

Rubi was aghast and feared she was already dead. *Death,*
he thought, *an ill-lit corridor with all its greater rooms
beyond.*

Rushing over to her side, he ran his arm under her head and
gently pulled her up. She was ashen, tallow. Suddenly, all
their arguments seemed trivial.

"My God, Doris, what have you done?" he said.

Her eyes slowly opened as if coming out of a mist and then
she slumped back to the bed.

Paramedics arrived, Doris was bandaged, and rushed to the
hospital, where she stayed for a single night. The following
day, Rubi signed her into a "rest cure resort" in Italy under a
pseudonym. When she got out two weeks later, she flew to
New York to talk with her lawyer about a divorce.

Later that month, after her return, while the couple was at
lunch, a man in a dark suit appeared at their table with divorce
papers.

Rubi was enraged, as he jumped to his feet. "All right then! Let's take advantage of this shyster's appearance."

An agreement was signed soon after, and it was a generous one. Rubi, despite the prenuptial agreement, received the 17th century mansion in Paris, a stable of polo ponies, $500,000 in cash, the converted B-25, and several Italian sports cars. It is rumored he was also given an annual stipend of $25,000 for life, until he remarried.

On October 27, the divorce was officially declared. A friend later asked Rubi why he had married Duke.

"What I did," Rubi said, "is better than what most would. They go out with a girl from a good family. They take all her money and then they leave. The difference with me is that I married her, gave her the best time in the world and when I left, I left her richer than ever before."

However, they continued to see one another for another two years and it was even rumored that they had secretly re-wed in Paris, though that was never substantiated. Neither could seem to get the other out of his or her blood.

Rubi once philosophized after a friend asked him about Doris:

Marriage does something to a love affair. It takes something delightful out of it. There is a piquancy about love—when two people know they can leave each other—that never exists inside the circle of a wedding ring. It can look appealing from a distance until you are in it, and then the horrors of the institution scream at you.

Marriage is for women—ugly women. It makes no sense for a man.

Socialite C. Z. Guest, a longtime friend of Duke's, later said that the heiress never said a bad word about Rubi—ever. And when she died in New Jersey in 1993, next to her bed were only two framed photographs—one of her then boyfriend, Louis Broomfield, the other a picture of Rubi.

Several years ago, on one of our visits to Duke's Rhode Island mansion, Isabella and I were looking for other clues to Rubi's story.

It was an enormous mansion complete with tour guides who worked full time, yet no one used it anymore. The young guide took us through each room, and every one of them elicited some story about Doris but no references to Rubi; that is, until we got to her bedroom. There on the nightstand were two pictures in beautiful ornate silver frames. I didn't recognize one of the men, but the other picture was most definitely Rubi.

I asked the guide about the two pictures. She told us that it was rumored these were the only two men Doris had ever truly loved.

Following the divorce, Doris moved back into her home in Reno and Rubi flew his valet to Buenos Aires to collect the rest of his belongings. Among them was a stamp collection reportedly worth a quarter of a million dollars.

It is also interesting to note that Rubi may have been called a gigolo, but this had been his second golden opportunity to create a powerful, lasting position for himself, an annuity of sorts, either in a political sense or just in a business sense and yet, he did not act on the opportunity.

The OSS had nothing to worry about apparently, because none of that type of thing took place. Had he played his cards the way some thought he should have, he could have commanded an enormous amount of influence and power. So, what was his true motivation? Was it love?

'I Jilted Rubi, Then He Hit Me,' Zsa Zsa Says

By LOUELLA O. PARSONS,
IS Motion Picture Editor.

HOLLYWOOD, Dec. 30.—Porfirio Rubirosa's parting gift Zsa Zsa Gabor was a black eye and a bruised elbow.

Said Zsa Zsa:

"He begged me to marry him and when I wouldn't he hit me. He hit me because I jilted him—he

believe I meant it," Zsa Zsa told me.

She didn't know, she said, whether Rubirosa's fist was open or clenched.

Zsa Zsa said he followed

This galleon, Nuestra Senora de la Concepcion, had been en route from Mexico to Europe by way of Havana. Korganoff said it was laden with gold and silver ingots, jewelry, and all manner of gold pieces. All of the treasure was destined for the King of Spain.

– Porfirio Rubirosa

On another front, during Rubi's subsequent tenure in Argentina (1945-48), Cuba joined the United Nations, Fidel Castro entered the University of Havana, and famed mobster Lucky Lucianno called a summit in Havana.

Attendees at the summit at the Hotel Nacional, owned by famed mob character, Meyer Lansky, included: Meyer, Frank Costello, Tommy Lucchese, Vito Genoveses, Joe Bonanno, Santo Trafficante, and Moe Dalitz. Lansky, one of the top racketeers in the country, also brought the cream of Reno and New York gamblers to Cuba.

Among the topics discussed was the assassination of Bugsy Siegel. Coincidentally, Frank Sinatra made his singing debut that year in Havana.

Many years before, Cuba had already developed the reputation of the playground of the eastern United States. With the end of World War II, Cuba awaited only the "mending" of the U.S. economy to resume its position as the international playground to the wealthy, to Hollywood celebrities, and to the mob.

Meyer Lansky's dreams for Cuba had already incubated in Las Vegas with his former partner Benny Siegel's venture, the Flamingo Hotel.

Batista was then in the Cuban senate, but later as president, he formulated a partnership with Lansky, which was a government gold mine, and Nevada-style casinos in an unregulated (except for the government) environment, began to flourish.

The mob came to Cuba prior to Batista. When Batista came to power, he was backed by the U.S. Then Castro took over in a coup, at which point Cuba became a threat to the United States. That threat would eventually include the Dominican Republic because of Trujillo's hatred of communism and his distrust of Castro.

In January of 1949, Trujillo appointed Rubi Minister to Rome. Since the distance between Rome and Paris is short, Rubi found it easy to move between the mansion and the embassy.

He loved the home and seemed to relish living there alone without Duke, with the exception of the "company" of the servants. It became the scene of many torrid affairs. It was a 20,000 square foot, three-story bachelor pad playhouse where one woman would be entering through the porch as another was judiciously being escorted out through the gardens. Later, a gorgeous playmate would be descending one of the staircases, while another would be escorted to a nearby sitting room.

Celebrated guests included Rita Hayworth and Tina Onassis, wife of Greek shipping billionaire Aristotle Onassis, who of course went on to marry Jackie Kennedy.

When he was needed in Rome, Rubi would fly the Bomber and eventually during one of these trips, he was forced to make another emergency landing. It was said that the second incident made him so nervous, that immediately upon his return he took one of his maids to bed to calm himself.

✗

In 1951, Rubi met King Farouk in a bar in Cairo, compliments of two beautiful women Rubi had known for some time. The two hit it off right away, Rubi immediately charming the royal. The older Farouk's philandering presaged Rubi's, so there was no lack of common ground.

Farouk, like Rubi, wasn't particularly handsome. He was short of stature and pudgy, even obese, but nevertheless maintained a perma-tan and considered the pursuit of women, racing Ferraris, and playing polo as an occupation in itself.

In those days, the quintessential bon vivant was a man named Gunter Sachs, who was once married to Brigitte Bardot. He always held that there were only 12 genuine playboys in the world (himself included), who "lived what actors acted."

Farouk

The pudgy playboy king

These men included: Alain Delon; Roger Vadim, the French movie director, who also married Bardot; Porfirio Rubirosa; Prince Aly Khan; Prince Dado; Ruspoli; King Farouk; the Marquis de Portago; and the Fiat heir, Gianni Agnelli; Eddie Fisher; Nicky Hilton;

and the mining magnate, Francisco Pignatari, all of whom "operated" from the '40s through the '70s.

Perhaps Rubi was one of only three on the list that people still remember.

For the month after the two men met, Rubi and Farouk had fun staying up until five in the morning, the principle playgrounds being Deauville in France, Monte Carlo, and St. Moritz.

Two women often accompanied Farouk: Honeychite, an American, and oddly, an Australian beauty named Phil. The four would often revel in the nightclubs of Cairo, which were far more subdued in the Muslim world than the hot spots Rubi was accustomed to in Paris.

Though Farouk was a large, plump man, he was not a drinker, nor much of an eater. Apparently, his obesity was the result of a glandular irregularity.

His other glands worked quite well, however, and the two men inhaled the many delights that their two companions bestowed upon them.

The contact allowed Rubi to get to know the King well and he found him to be surprisingly complex and unpredictable.

Once, when Rubi had been seriously injured during a polo match for the King's Cup, he was taken to the hospital to tend to a battered nose and head. Two hours later, Farouk came to see him and said, "Poor Rubi. You're going to be terribly bored here. I will find you some suitable company."

Late that night, as Rubi languished in his hospital bed, a beautiful French singer appeared in his room.

"Good evening," she said. "His majesty sent me here. It seems unusual because he is such a jealous man but he's told me you were injured playing polo and that I was to keep you company."

Rubi smiled, but could barely move, constricted by all the bandages and bruising.

What a stunning woman she was. An Arab with olive skin the texture of silk. She smelled of incense and herbs. I could feel myself becoming aroused quickly. I could barely move my other limbs, one of them was pressing tight to my gown and the bed sheets. It was painful and delicious all at once.

Sensing this, she drew closer to me and stroked my brow with her soft hand, then took my face in both hands, caressed me, and began to kiss me passionately. Her other hand slid surreptitiously under the sheets.

My breathing quickened as I responded. I wanted to devour her, but the bandages were like a straightjacket and I was helpless to consummate her affection, at least in the manner she intended.

I will forever remember that missed opportunity. The memory of her often crept into my mind when I was in dangerous situations later. I did not ever want to find myself indisposed at a time like that.

✗

Several days later, Rubi was invited to dinner aboard the King's yacht in Alexandria. Rubi thanked the King, but declined, stating he'd already committed to another dinner with his fellow polo players.

The King immediately proposed a change of plans. "Very well, then, bring your team with you and join us for coffee. I will send my Chief of the Air Force to transport you."

The next day, Rubi and his team flew to the King's desert "tent" on a giant Sikorsky helicopter, flying over the pyramids and landing at Farouk Airport—all for a few cups of coffee and some lively conversation.

In 1952, King Farouk was forced to abdicate the Egyptian throne and console himself with yachting and gambling in Monaco. Rubi continued to maintain a warm relationship with his friend for many years thereafter.

The same year that Farouk "retired," Rubi got the lost treasure bug and decided to hunt for sunken treasure off the north coast of the Dominican Republic. He was single, without a job or a particular love mate, and was once again bored, though he had dabbled in a fishery in the Congo and had purchased land on the French Atlantic coast and some fishing boats. However, those small businesses were turned over to a manager. Rubi lacked the enthusiasm for anything so mundane as fishing.

That year, Rubi met a man in a bar who insisted on introducing him to a man named Korganoff, who was obsessed with the story of a treasure lying at the bottom of the Caribbean Sea on the north coast of the Dominican Republic. He told Rubi that the introduction would be the perfect opportunity for mystery, adventure, and gamesmanship. Rubi had one thing to say, "Bring me your Korganoff."

The next day, the man arrived at my door. He was much younger than I had envisioned, about 30 perhaps, almost adolescent looking. He was tall, blonde, and fidgeted about in a nervous mood. Under his arm was a leather-bound bundle of papers, which he immediately proceeded to spread out on the coffee table. There were maps, texts, nautical documents, old-fashioned notebooks, and a jumble of miscellaneous notes.

Without the formalities of small talk, he set about telling his formidable story, as excited as a child on Christmas Eve. Within the first few minutes, I was enthralled with his tale, even possessed by his story.

The short version is this: On October 2, 1639, a Spanish galleon weighing 350 tons was lying off the north coast of the Dominican Republic, over some coral reefs in an inlet called Banco de la Plata.

This galleon, Nuestra Senora de la Concepcion, had been en route from Mexico to Europe by way of Havana. Korganoff said it was laden with gold and silver ingots, jewelry, and all manner of gold pieces. All of the treasure was destined for the King of Spain. However, the galleon struck the coral reef but did not sink immediately, giving most of the crew time to throw a skiff into the water and escape.

Since the ship was still afloat, the captain and his men made their way to shore and then traversed the width of the entire island to report the wreck to someone in the capital.

Noting the magnitude of the treasure, there was no lack of volunteers for a rescue mission and so forty men set out across the island back to Banco de la Plata. By the time they arrived on the shore, there was no sign of the ship. Several expeditions over the next year failed to recover any treasure, nor was any sign of the galleon ever discovered.

Two hundred years later (1839), a British carpenter, William Phips, who was living in America—according to Korganoff—had access to records and archives in Spain relating to the ship. He obtained some financial backing and assembled a crew to retrieve the treasure. He and his crew spent two miserable years searching. Some of his sailors mutinied and were sent to prison in the Dominican. Phips was also robbed and threatened and had to purchase a second ship. One day lady luck did smile upon him.

While working on deck, he saw some flowering coral and sent one of the sailors to investigate. In moments, the swimmer returned to the surface shouting that he'd found something. More men were sent overboard and shortly they reported finding the shell of the galleon and part of the bridge, but no storeroom where the cargo would have been stored.

According to Korganoff, Phips had made detailed notes in his log pinpointing the location of the galleon, even making sketches of the large coral rock that had been the galleon's demise.

Since there was only one rock of this magnitude visible at low tide, Korganoff had determined that scuba divers wouldn't even be needed to target the location. In short, it would be easy pickings and we would both be extremely rich.

In hindsight, I can see that easy riches dazzled and blinded me. The clues that I was dealing with an exuberant youth, with little experience, eluded me in my greed.

I did not have 26 days to help them find a boat, obtain the dynamite, hire on a crew, and all the other details. I left that to this young man. Later, I flew to Banco de la Plata where 50,000 square meters of flowering coral is nirvana for scuba divers. It is one of the most beautiful seaside areas in the Dominican Republic—also quite dangerous.

My first contact with the crew and Korganoff was discouraging. No sooner had I met the captain, a man named Prejean, than he asked if I had a package for him. I replied yes and handed him a letter and box. He grabbed them from me, as a man stranded in the desert would lurch at another with a canteen of water.

The fool was love struck and the letter was from the girl he'd left in France. He, also, was quite young and immediately disappeared below deck to dwell on the words of his girlfriend.

It was apparent that we were in trouble already. My fate was in the hands of two inexperienced youth, one who was love struck and completely disengaged from the task, the other a hyper-manic with visions of sugar plums, or rather gold dubloons, dancing in his head.

These were not the daring young sailors or decisive men of action I might have expected to encounter.

Of course, mistake after mistake ensued. No sooner had we set sail than we crashed into the only schooner moored in the inlet—a nearly impossible feat. The propeller got tangled in the schooner's ropes.

Several days later, our lovesick young captain abruptly abandoned us to return to France, and the second hand took over. We finally left on March 16; at least the weather was beautiful. After navigating for 15 hours on a sparkling, limpid sea, we arrived near the site in Banco de la Plata.

Huge multicolored coral was illuminated by the sea and sun. It was an astounding sight. One of the sailors climbed the mast and helped us navigate through the reef.

Once we were close, we dropped anchor and for several days, we searched in rubber rafts, covered with lotion to try to protect us from the broiling sun. Even I, with fairly dark skin, became chafed and sunburned. The water was an azure color but as clear as a glass of water as we searched for the rock that Phips had drawn.

My job was to ward off sharks with my pistola, as the divers scoured the reefs. They were planting dynamite to loosen up large sections of coral, hoping to expose the galleon.

After about a week of blowing up sections of reef, we spotted what could have been said to be a large rock. Korganoff went crazy, running about the deck, shouting, "We're going to find it! We're going to find it!" But, of course, we did not—at least not immediately.

I had been in a daze for the past several weeks, but my good logic softened with the prospects of sudden, easy riches. Now, I realized that this was going to be more difficult than I'd imagined. I constructed a canopy on the deck, under which I laid on an air mattress. Within arm's reach, I kept a cooler for my beer, listening to concerts from Miami on the radio, and at least enjoying the warmth, while all around me the continual rumble of the explosions of dynamite disturbed the air and all the creatures around us.

Throughout the first few days, the crew, when some of them weren't in the water, were gulping down great quantities of wine, and I watched as their brains began to fail. I soon realized that we had no chance of success unless we got rid of this sorry excuse for a crew.

I told Korganoff that we would have to go to a port called

Long Beach and locate a new crew, which I did. In my absence, Korganoff called me to say the crew was completely out of control. "They're all drunk and crazy and they're ripping up the bars in town."

Before I could arrive and intervene, soldiers arrived at the port and arrested the entire crew. Soon afterward, they were all deported to France and we were essentially back to square one.

I assembled a Dominican crew this time—myself—fearing my entire investment of $250,000 was about to be lost. They were to take the ship back for needed repairs (plundering by the drunken previous crew), but that area of the coast was dangerous and a storm began to brew soon after they started their journey.

En route, the vessel hit a reef. The crew was able to save themselves, but not the boat. I gritted my teeth at the news, took a deep breath, and pledged I would not give up. Within a few days, I had rented a sailboat and hired on a captain and soon he, a crewmember, Korganoff, and I were back out at the reef near the buoy that Korganoff had fortunately set prior to the mutiny.

All that was left was to continue the search. At that point, I had no choice. We circled the area for two days and then I had business to attend to in Paris.

"What are you saying?" Korganoff asked in disbelief.

I'm saying, I have to leave. If anything happens, call me in Paris and I'll be on the first plane back. I cannot, however, stay here now.

I had only been in Paris three days when the call came. It was Korganoff and he was beside himself—so much so, that he could hardly speak.

"I've, I've found it," he said, nearly breathless.

Are you sure? Are you sure? I drilled him.

When I returned to the boat two days later, Korganoff told me that he'd spotted the shell of the galleon about 20 meters *below the spot where the boat was anchored, and he had not told the crew.*

"I saw it, I tell you. The distinct shape of the bow." He even drew a sketch for me.

Okay, in the morning, we begin, I told him. That night was marvelously calm and though it was dark, the sky seemed a deep shade of gold. I slept on deck on the air mattress, exhausted, I nodded off at 9 o'clock.

Several hours later, I was awakened by a whistling wind. Sitting up, I could see white choppy crests of waves being whipped up by a suddenly surging wind. It was an odd feeling, a sort of calm, mixed with a budding anger. At once, I knew what it meant. We were being visited by either a hurricane or a tornado. I remembered the signs from my youth.

The crew was huddled at the back of the boat, instinctively knowing something bad was about to happen. It doesn't take long after the initial signs of a tornado before the seas become whipped to a frenzy, and that is exactly what happened.

The boat began to be tossed about furiously; the sky grew dark and forbidding; and the small choppy sea became an angry, furious adversary.

Waves turned to walls of water 20 feet high, and our small boat began to be tossed about like a wine cork in a washing machine.

Suddenly, the anchor chain snapped and all hell broke loose. We were adrift with no ability to navigate; it was too dark to motor through the reefs.

That entire night, we were at the mercy of the effects of a horrendous tornado that had punished great portions of the Caribbean. The crew, Korganoff, and I tied ourselves to the rails with heavy ropes and just prayed we would be spared.

The tornado never did hit land but came close enough to nearly kill us all. In the morning, an odd serenity returned. The seas were once again calm, with not even a hint of a breeze. There wasn't a cloud in the sky, which was the brightest blue

I'd ever seen. Then one of the crew pointed to the north. I turned my head to see the most spectacular rainbow I'd ever seen. It was as if God had been angry with me, or perhaps the entire Caribbean, but then had forgiven us and offered up a bouquet of flowers.

Once safely on land, I realized my quest was not meant to be. I would never again go near Banco de la Plata. For all my efforts and near death experience, all I had to show for my treasure hunt was an empty bank account—$250,000, gone. I might as well have thrown it into a bonfire.

(**Note:** In 1979, a North American investigator from Seaquest International made an interesting discovery in Banco de la Plata, including large amounts of coins, silver ingots, candelabras, ornate jars and galipots, crystal glasses, and other items, which were put on display at the Museo de las Cas Reales in Santo Domingo.

(An agreement was struck with the Dominican Republic stating that any treasures found would be divided evenly between the Dominican and Seaquest. To the date of this writing (2005), no other gold, silver, or jewelry has been found.)

With the adventure of treasure hunting out of his blood, Rubi returned to Paris. Still in Trujillo's good graces, he could simply ask for money whenever he needed it and the president would send him a check. He was considered the best public relations that money could buy for the Dominican Republic.

A typical day for Rubi was to sleep until noon. After coffee, he would usually drive one of the Ferraris over to the Bagatelle Polo Club and exercise his ponies until about six. There was no mistaking him—he was the only rider who wore a smoking jacket and scarf.

After wearing down several ponies, Rubi would meet with friends in the Club and begin his requisite drinking. They said he could usually finish off a quart of scotch by himself.

Drinking with friends would go on until well after midnight and then around 2:00 a.m., the "petit cochon" (little pig)—the animal that sleeps inside every man's brain, according to Rubi—would wake up and then it was time for the women.

Rubi was a creature of habit. Most every night he could be found at the legendary Jimmy's disco in Paris.

The owner, Regine, said that when he came in, the place completely changed. He was magnetic, even magical.

Rubi's usual approach to meeting a new woman was simply to do nothing. For the most part, his reputation preceded him. When it didn't, he would act aloof, often sitting in a large leather booth all alone with a bottle of 12-year-old Scotch and a single glass, pulling long, slow drags from one of his more expensive, unfiltered American cigarettes—usually one of Duke's brands.

He never approached the women. The wait was never more than a few minutes because the eyes of every woman in the club were glued to him.

The women would just light up with energy and soon there would be three or four of them fawning all over him. Oftentimes, they would literally drag him out onto the dance floor—sometimes into the ladies room.

Oddly, though he could have his choice of any woman, he had a weakness for the plump ones. At times, he was reported to have made love in most of the areas of the club, including the wine cellar, the ladies room, and even behind the bar.

I was practically wallpaper at Jimmy's, even to the extent that one evening, I stayed so late, he asked me to close up. I had been dancing most of the night with a fetching young Swedish girl, no more that 20 years old.

When you're not married, there is a fitful pleasure you get by not having to conform to a wife's wishes. Freedom brings this pleasure, not in fits, but in flurries. Such was this evening.

The girl, I believe her name was Galene, was perfect, at least through the haze of the Scotch—her eyes, skin, hair all seemed somehow baroque, saturated with color. It was as if all of her features acted as a frame for her desire for me.

Unlike a wife, she could not, would not, spot my flaws. She could not see the emptiness that sometimes resides within me, nor the spiritual deprivation that I sometimes accused myself of—only desire—in this case a torch of wishing.

I was taken not only by her seductive looks, but also by her naiveté and her inability to see anything but a hero in front of her.

We remained seated together in a booth, as Jimmy, the manager, passed by, dropped an extra key in my hand, smiled a knowing smile, waved, and locked the front door behind him.

The light from the single candle on our table illuminated all that we both wanted to see and no more. She leaned into me now, a final soft ballad playing on the jukebox. I pressed my lips to her moist mouth and reveled in her liquids as she did in mine.

Placing my arm around her waist gently, I pulled the two of us from the booth and then began to dance slowly with her.

I reached under her skirt, wrapped my arms around her thighs, and hoisted her onto the bar.

She was breathing and crying so loud, I thought someone might hear us from down the street. When we were spent, which was about two hours later, we departed, not remembering to lock the door, or even wipe down the bar.

In addition to his obvious physical endowment, Rubi had the one luxury that allowed him his phenomenal stamina that most people did not enjoy—time. He could drink and womanize until dawn because he didn't have to wake up at any particular time. In fact, there were many times that he stayed in bed the entire day. There is an old saying, "You can have the nights, or you can have the days, but you can't have both."

Rubi's calling card was simple—a single red rose along with a card that read, "To the most beautiful of women." And his charm wasn't limited to his sex appeal; he took pains to maintain an elegant demeanor and appearance, always dressed in silk or linen in the warm months and the finest woolen suits in the cooler seasons.

He seemed to have a natural sense of design and fashion and always chose just the right cologne with great care and not too much of it.

He was much like a Latin Fred Astaire who seemed to glide on air and always make the right gestures. At the age of 44, he was really just starting to come into his own.

Shortly after his treasure hunting adventure, in 1952, Rubi found himself embroiled in another kind of escapade—this time, not entirely of his own making: a tryst that would jeopardize his diplomatic career.

While serving as Charge d' Affairs, Richard Reynolds (R.J.), the heir to the Reynolds Tobacco fortune, accused Rubi of having a love affair with his wife. Rubi defended himself by explaining that he and Marianne Reynolds had merely exchanged some words. However, according to several media accounts, wherever the Reynolds' yacht docked, Rubirosa was never far away. It was reported that Marianne Reynolds, a former actress, was unhappily married to R.J. Reynolds.

Years later, Patrick Reynolds, Marianne, and R.J.'s son stated that Rubi never really meant that much to his mother, and he had asked her before she died why she'd had an affair with him.

She replied that she'd been standing on the deck of one of the largest boats in the world (her husband's yacht), wearing a beautiful gown and dripping with diamonds, emeralds, and rubies, but that she was really little more than a prisoner because, "Every night at five, your father passed out drunk. And, when Rubi came calling, asking me to join him for dinner, by God, I went."

Patrick Reynolds told the press that his mother consummated the affair in Paris, but that it only lasted long enough for his father to hire a detective to catch the couple in the act, which the detective did.

Walter Winchell reported the affair and Patrick believed that naming Rubi saved his father a couple of million dollars in the divorce settlement.

Not long after that affair, the British golfer, Robert Sweeny, would also obtain a divorce alleging that his wife, Joanne Connelly had committed adultery with Rubirosa.

In this instance, Rubi stated that he was just being used by a couple that already wanted a divorce. He also stated that it was Joanne who was the aggressor and that she had actually seduced him.

I was a fool and it cost me dearly. One night while I was with friends at the Embassy Club in London, two women came in and sat at a nearby table. One of them was Joanne Connelly who I'd known socially for years.

I immediately felt it proper and indeed, thoughtful, to pay my respects, as you would with any old friend.

When I approached the table, her eyes lit up and she gave me a bit of a coy smile and then introduced her friend.

"Rubi, please sit and have a drink with us," she said.

Before I accepted, I went back to my table and asked my friends to give me a few moments with an old friend and then told them I would return.

When I came back to the table, there were three chilled, neat martinis sitting there.

After we had finished the drinks, I tried to dismiss myself, but Joanne would have none of it.

"Rubi, I would like you to come with me," she said.

This was totally unexpected. I didn't have a car, and I didn't want to leave my friends.

I'm sorry Joanne. I can't leave my friends, I responded, trying to beg off.

Then she shot me an expression that can only be described as a combination of pleading and seduction, with a pinch of disappointment mixed in.

I gently raised her hand in mine, brought it to my lips, and kissed it, saying, Really, Joanne, I mustn't do this to my friends.

That was it. I returned to my table.

Joanne continued to chat with her friend and over the next few minutes also continued to smile and wave at me, which I kept trying to politely acknowledge.

Just as my friends and I were settling the tab and about to leave, Joanne approached me again and in front of my friends, nearly demanded that I accompany her. What could I do? I excused myself, telling my friends I would return, and then I walked out to the front of the hotel where I bid her adieu.

She would have none of it.

"If you were truly a gentleman, Rubi, you would at least escort me to the elevator."

I could feel it instantly. I was being drawn ever so deviously into the spider's web, but didn't yet know my feet were sticky.

Of course, when we reached the elevator, her plea to at least accompany her to her door, was the next plea. At that point, I felt I would be insulting her by not doing so.

I had already anticipated her next move. I knew that when we got to her door, she would invite me in for a drink.

Knowing I would not be able to wriggle out of it, I would say yes, but just one and then having that one aperitif, I would inexorably excuse myself to my now, long-waiting friends who would surely, by then, have thought me a bore.

Even with my quick-witted plan firmly in place, I could not have anticipated her next move. It was like a game of chess between a Russian Grand Master and a six-year old checkers player.

Exiting the elevator on the 5th floor, we walked side by side down the long, ornately decorated hall, coming upon her door. As anticipated, she said, "Rubi, you simply must come in for just one drink. What could a couple of more minutes hurt?"

Joanne, I really must attend to my friends. They've come all the way from Paris to visit me, I said, knowing I was going to give into the one drink anyway.

"I won't have it. Please, Rubi. It is so lonely here by myself. Just one nightcap. A small cognac, perhaps?"

The cognac never arrived. Instead, as I sat on the heavy-quilted sofa, Joanne excused herself, saying she had to make one quick phone call. When she returned in a few moments, she was dressed in a see-through silk negligee, cut nearly to her waist. I had to admit, she was quite alluring.

At that point, I knew that I was in trouble. I began to stand up slowly, this time fully determined to leave, when she came gliding across the room and literally threw herself into my lap.

There she laid, stretched out like a cat, purring at me, stroking my cheek with her hand.

I froze, not knowing how to extricate myself without great difficulty. Then, unexpectedly, the door opened. There had been no sound of a key turning, so it took me quite by surprise.

Standing there like a scolding mother was a maid in a prim white and black uniform, hands on hips, glaring at us.

I quickly pushed at Joanne's shoulders, slid her to the side, and jumped up.

Joanne. Really now. I have to go, I said.

And that is all that I said as I fled out and down the hall, returning to my still waiting friends. From there, the four of us went to another club where I shared my predicament with them as we all had a great laugh.

Rubi at the wheel
Speed & danger excited him.
He excited rich women.

Several days later, while I was in Paris, I picked up a morning paper and there in 72-point type headlines was the story of the Connelly divorce, listing me as the cause. I had been named as the responsible party for the adultery that was supposedly committed.

My first thoughts raced back to that maid, who had so easily entered the room. How propitious.

✗

Rubi was formally named as the cause of the divorce and because the case was held in a British court, by law, Rubi was sentenced to pay all the fees prescribed. In the end, he felt he was a pawn and just the victim of a wisely planned ploy.

Shortly after this second indictment, Trujillo, in a fit of anger, ordered Rubi removed from his position and published his intentions in an American newspaper, stating it was a punishment for the diplomat's deplorable behavior.

Rubi would no longer be pulling down his $600 a month

salary, but more importantly, once again, he would have to get by without the magic of his diplomatic passport.

Did Trujillo really take umbrage with Rubi's behavior, or was he just asserting once again, that *he* was the one and only benefactor, the only boss?

✗

That same year, Fidel Castro, the future American and Dominican nemesis, two years out of law school, ran for Congress under the Orthodox Party banner.

In March, Batista took over again, this time in a bloodless coup d'etat. The elections, which were three months away, were canceled and the United States officially recognized the Batista government.

In 1953, Rubi flew to New York before New Year's Eve, taking up residence at the Plaza Hotel. When he entered the elevator in the afternoon of New Year's Day, he was immediately taken aback by a stunning blonde, a Hungarian actress who had just been to the premiere of her successful movie, *Moulin Rouge.*

It was Zsa Zsa Gabor.

Rubi didn't know who she was, but he was nearly breathless with her beauty.

On the other hand, Gabor knew instantly who Rubi was: Machismo incarnate, a legend at the age of 20. Married to Doris Duke; playboy, polo player, racecar driver; Casanova, Don Juan, and a charmer:

"I knew all this, but none of it impressed me." Gabor wrote. "After all, I was the ex-Mrs. Conrad Hilton, the ex-Mrs. Burhan Belge, Ataturk's love and above all, George Sanders' current wife.

"I'd been involved with some of the most charismatic men in the world. The myth of Porfirio Rubirosa, I told myself, had nothing to do with me except that when I had threatened George that I might go to bed with Rubi—he had momentarily dropped his guard and gone pale. No, Porfirio Rubirosa interested me only on account of George and not on account of himself."

The elevator encounter was brief and simple—an exchange of pleasantries and a gesture by Rubi for her to step out first. Then she disappeared down the long hallway into her room.

Gabor laid down for a nap, but Rubi kept busy for the next hour. When she awoke, notwithstanding his penchant for sending a single rose, Zsa Zsa's room was filled with hundreds of flowers—roses, gardenias, lilies, and lilacs. The smell was intoxicating. It was like awakening from a dream at a florist's.

A white card lay on the table in the foyer. Gabor opened it and read,

"Don Porfirio Rubirosa, Minister Plenipotentiary of the Dominican Republic. My greetings for the most beautiful of women."

Zsa Zsa Gabor
Rubi was a man who got what he wanted

It was an invitation to meet in the Persian Room downstairs for drinks.

At first, she dismissed the flowers and the invitation, but had a change of mind as the sun began to set.

"I still wasn't impressed by Rubi or the idea of meeting him, but I accepted, feeling miserable and alone without George by my side."

As Zsa Zsa strolled into the bar with her mother as an escort, Rubi stood up and took the hand of Gabor's mother first, held it gently and then kissed it.

"I am Porfirio Rubirosa," he said to her mother. "I am proud to make your acquaintance." Then, just as quickly, he took Zsa Zsa's hand and then gestured for the two to be seated.

Zsa Zsa wrote later in her book *One Lifetime is Not Enough*:

"In that moment, Rubi finally impressed me. He was dark, magnetic, as mysterious, cool, and composed as Conrad Hilton, and equally urbane as George Sanders. Before we even touched, he mesmerized me."

Rubi and Zsa Zsa spent that first night at the Plaza together and from that moment on, she knew she did not ever want to leave him, even though she was madly in love with her husband.

The following day, Rubi left for Paris and Zsa Zsa went to Rome. Apparently, her husband, who was in Italy filming a movie, sensed something was amiss. He wanted her to join him immediately.

After a few weeks in Rome, Zsa Zsa flew to Las Vegas where she received a call, not moments after arriving, the unmistakable voice of Rubirosa.

"My Cherie, tomorrow I have the night off. How about seeing each other? I'll fly from Paris through Mexico, spend the night with you and then fly back to Paris in the morning," which he did, a 4,000 mile trip for a single date!

For months afterward, Rubi showered Gabor with flowers, telegrams, and endless phone calls. The fact that she was married never dulled his ardor. Finally, one of the missives was intercepted by Sanders, who simply read the card, walked over to Zsa Zsa, and with a rye smile congratulated his wife for conquering the great Latin lover.

Zsa Zsa was horrified and insisted there was nothing between her and Rubi. Sanders, who always seemed to be in a pleasant, peaceful mood, suggested that she answer the note. When she ignored him, George wrote back to Rubi on her behalf, expressing her love and impatience to be with him again.

Several weeks later, a call came from Paris asking that she consider a new French production. It was perfect timing. Zsa Zsa left immediately and was surprised when Rubi met her at the airport.

Of course, Rubi put her up in his mansion and even she was impressed with the lodgings and the constant stream of celebrities and dignitaries. She was intoxicated, "under a sexual trance," as she put it, with the spell Rubi seemed to have over her.

His mansion reminded Gabor of her lover, the Turkish president Ataturk's secret hideaway in Ankara—a romantic dream, an oasis of sensuality, a place where they would spend hours making love, and Rubi would play soft music, even bathe and dress her.

While she worked on the film, Rubi played polo, attending sporadically to his diplomatic duties.

The two played for months in 1953, in Paris, Cannes, Deauville, and Rome and all the while Rubi begged her to divorce Sanders and marry him. Notwithstanding her feelings for Rubi, she was torn. She loved both men. She found herself caught in an agonizingly exquisite dilemma.

When Zsa Zsa was finished filming, the two would sleep till noon every day and then rise and drive Rubi's Mercedes into the city, cruising down the Champs Elyseses and stopping to eat oysters for breakfast.

Then they would adjourn to the Bagatelle where he would play polo and she would watch. He even bought her a small polo pony that they called "Little Sister," and taught her how to ride.

After the dynamic duo was through riding, they would return to the mansion and spend hours making love before they dressed for cocktails and dinner at Maxim's and then usually on to Jimmy's disco.

She adored Rubi and he loved her, but the affair was a roller coaster ride with frequent fights. After one particularly nasty argument, Zsa Zsa decided to return home. She arrived, fearful of her husband's wrath, knowing her affair had been publicized around the world. His only comment was, "Darling, sexual passion lasts only two years. You'll be back with Daddy. You've made me look rather ridiculous with your Rubirosa affair. But I forgive you because you always make me laugh."

That evening they went to the Bel-Air Hotel for dinner, and Zsa Zsa remarked that she thought George was putting on weight.

"Not at all," he retorted. "It is just that your lover in Paris is much slimmer than I."

Despite Sanders' apparent ease with the affair, he filed for divorce that year (1953). Zsa Zsa was devastated. She'd had the affair, but she was still very much in love with Sanders.

"We were like two children," she wrote in her autobiography. "Pleasure-seeking, hedonistic, perhaps spoiled and selfish."

Later that year, the Frontier Hotel in Las Vegas offered Zsa Zsa and

'Look how unhappy they look!' Zsa Zsa Gabor laughs as she is handed a photo of the Rubirosa-Hutton wedding. The Hungarian beauty sniffed she was 'very, very happy' that Rubirosa got married because now he could pay her the $5600 hotel bill he owed her.

her sisters, Eva and Magda, a nightclub act. The act was to begin on Christmas day—the same day Rubi arrived in Las Vegas to propose marriage. When she declined, he was so angry he punched her. She showed up the next day to rehearsals with a black eyepatch, announcing to reporters and photographers that she had jilted him and in his subsequent rage, he had hit her in the eye.

The ensuing pictures were all over the tabloids for weeks. Enjoying the attention, even under the circumstances, she chose to wear the eye patch for a week after the bruise went away, for the sake of publicity. "The fact that he hit me proves that he loves me," she said. "A woman who has never been hit by a man has never been loved."

The press ate it up.

Having been rebuffed, Rubi confessed that he had met a new woman. Hearing the news, Zsa Zsa had a flashback, remembering Deauville, the elegant resort where she and Rubi had so recently played. As he rode his polo pony that day, she remembered a woman with binoculars trained on Rubi for nearly an hour. Later, the woman came to their table, blatantly flirted with him, and announced she would one day marry him.

How could Zsa Zsa ever forget the scene? It was Barbara Hutton, heir to the F.W. Woolworth fortune, nearly as rich as Doris Duke.

At the time, Zsa Zsa remembered just laughing, convinced that Rubi would always want her.

She remembered that morning vividly, when at four am, there came a clamorous noise of breaking glass in the other room. Suddenly, the French doors burst open and George Sanders appeared with two other men who were detectives.

Forgetting she was wearing only her diamond earrings, Zsa Zsa jumped out of bed. George, who hadn't seen her in months, stood mouth agape at his naked ex-wife. Rubi, also naked, bolted for the bathroom and locked himself in.

The two lovers' evening clothes were strewn over most of the room as well as draped over chairs. The scene shouted that a passionate and hasty disrobing had occurred.

The sweet but musty smell of love hung in the air as Zsa Zsa, standing defiantly, scolded George, wagging her finger at him with one hand, the other resting on her hip.

"How dare you burst in here like some Neanderthal," she said. Stark naked, she still maintained a haughty air.

Nevertheless, George ordered the photographer to work.

Pictures were snapped, notations made on pads of paper and then as the interlopers were about to depart, George walked gracefully and quietly over to the bathroom door, tapped on it lightly, and said, "Senor Rubirosa. You can't escape me that easily. I will see you in court."

After they left, Rubi emerged and the two, completely nonplused, continued to make love for several more hours.

Rubi was leaving the following day. When the sun was rising, he jumped up abruptly, got dressed, and said, "My darling, I have to leave you. I need money and Barbara Hutton has offered me five million dollars if I marry her. After I marry her, I'll come back to you in a few weeks."

Having lost a small fortune diving for sunken treasures and trying to support an affair with Zsa Zsa, who knew how to pour through money quickly, Rubi was truly broke for the first time since his young years in Paris after Flor had left him and he had been temporarily excommunicated by her father. Rubi's greatest fear had always been the threat of poverty. He could survive anything, as long as it wasn't labor or being broke.

I met Barbara in Deauville. I'd already known her for some time, since she'd been married to my friend Igor Troubetskoi. The summer I met her, she was staying at the Normandy

Hotel. We started seeing each other and having lunch, but she tired easily and needed to rest often, which cut our visits short on most occasions.

She'd had a son, Lance, by a previous marriage to an aristocrat, Count Kurt Von Reventhlow, and I often gave Lance polo lessons. Barbara had also been married to the actor Cary Grant. In all, she'd been married four times before we met.

The next time I saw her, she was in a hospital in New York. When I got there, she was undergoing treatment for some illness and during those visits, our friendship began to take a new direction; for whatever reason, we discovered a strong attraction to each other.

As she began to recover, she seemed to become a new, more invigorated woman—sensitive, intelligent, and cultured. Since the attraction was mutual, we agreed to get married in the winter of 1953.

The ceremony was at the Dominican Consulate in New York. When I arrived at the Hotel Pierre looking for her, hundreds of photographers and reporters crowded the lobby and spilled out into the street.

As I escorted her past the throngs, I heard one of the reporters say, "His next marriage will be to Fort Knox."

Flashbulbs popped incessantly, microphones were thrust into our faces, and Barbara seemed to reel in the claustrophobic atmosphere.

In the meantime, I tried to make Zsa Zsa understand. My design revolved around marriage, nevertheless, it was still a business plan. I needed money and not just a simple loan. I had every intention of coming back to Zsa Zsa, maybe not on a permanent basis, but at least for decent intervals, though, of course, I didn't say that to her.

I found Barbara's circumstances appealing and she was attractive in a vulnerable sort of way, so I began to visit her and to provide some companionship. She was in poor health *and seemed fragile, and so she greatly appreciated my visits, but I kept them very discreet.*

Among the many reported affairs he'd engaged in while in Hollywood, one notable mention was Rubi's fling with Joan Crawford ("Latin Lover. The Playboy of the Western World,". *Caribbean World* Magazine.)

"Rubi then tried Joan Crawford, with whom he spent a riotous weekend in Palms Springs. The lusty pair cleared the birds out of the trees for a few days and nights of their lovemaking,"

Joan Crawford
Not Rubi's type

writes Shaun Considine in his book about Crawford and Bette Davis.

"Crawford tried to make Rubi a movie star and introduced him to Hollywood producers. However, work permits and a career as a matinee idol never materialized. His relationship with Crawford was also doomed.

"Once, Rubi made the mistake of telling Crawford that she was stingy compared with his ex-wives. In their 10 days together, all that Joan had given him was a silver cigarette case and a gold money clip, with no cash included," wrote Considine.

"(On another occasion, a paltry gift had an accompanying card offhandedly signed: 'Amor, etcetera… Joan Crawford'.")

Rubi was even left to pay the hotel bill.

Barbara was beginning to grow very fond of Rubi and as her physical condition improved, they both became convinced they were meant for each other and that marriage was indeed on the horizon.

By this time, Rubi had grown to appreciate Barbara's intelligence and wit, which awakened a true affection in him. Barbara's temporary recovery revitalized her ardor as well.

An entry in one of her notebooks reads: "His lovemaking secret is that he practices an Egyptian technique called Imsak.

"No matter how aroused he becomes, he doesn't allow himself to complete the act.

"What he enjoys about it is the sense of control he achieves over his own body while exciting the woman beyond control, beyond the threshold."

Regardless of their desire for each other, and just prior to his marriage to Hutton, Rubi could not resist one final indiscretion. Trying to escape the many journalists, Rubi took flight to a bar in Manhattan where he met a barmaid and promptly disappeared with her for the rest of the day.

According to *Fortune* magazine, "Hutton was worth $25 million and apparently was determined to spend much of it on Rubi, so she began by matching Duke's gift."

A 400-acre citrus plantation in the Dominican Republic came next; 15 polo ponies, a Lancia car, ruby cufflinks, and a diamond stickpin followed.

Hutton's motives weren't without a degree of vanity. After all, if Doris Duke could have Rubi, why not her? Duke and Hutton were friends and for Hutton, this catch was part of the rivalry.

Everyone was dead set against the marriage. The general and customary concern was that Barbara's fortune would end up in Rubi's pockets. A torrent of negative Rubirosa articles followed with television and radio commentary. Barbara even received a phone call from her aunt begging her to call Doris Duke to learn everything she could about this man, which she did only to receive a glowing report that Rubi was an absolutely charming and perfect gentleman.

From the Hutton biography entitled *Poor Little Rich Girl*:

"However, the feeling among her friends and foes alike was that her decision to marry the Dominican playboy was, for her, another indulgence she was permitting herself, even in the face of certain disaster.

"Her ex-husband, Cary Grant, and her friend, Baron Gottfried von Cramm, sent telegrams imploring her to reconsider. Her uncle, E.F. Hutton, called and in an acerbic tone, not unlike her father's, said, 'Have you gone out of your mind, Barbara? Do you know what this man is? And do you realize what that makes you?'"

Rubi soon learned that Barbara was more frail than he thought, a woman prone to illness, often fighting off various lung infections. In fact, she spent a great deal of time in bed; but Rubi still saw her as someone who was smart, cultivated, and sensible, even though he tired of her illnesses quickly.

Problems with the upcoming wedding followed all the negative exhortations from Barbara's family and friends. Just days prior to the ceremony, it was discovered that the wedding would be illegal in New York because neither of them had obtained the requisite blood tests.

Rubi had the matter taken care of through the Dominican government, which, after his insistence, issued a proclamation and special decree that Miss Hutton was granted a Dominican citizenship. The wedding, therefore, could be held at the Dominican Consulate on Park Avenue in New York.

Upon hearing this news, Barbara's aunt collapsed and had to be rushed to the hospital.

Aunt Marjorie, thinking that a marriage approved under Dominican law, one in which Barbara also became an instant citizen of that country, simply fainted in disgust. Upon her release, she immediately contacted Barbara's lawyer in an effort to draft an agreement to cover Barbara's financials. Since Barbara technically controlled all the purse strings of that vast fortune, everyone in her family feared this union.

Rubi and Barbara
The bride carried a scotch and soda

The wedding was finally held on December 30, 1953—not at the Consulate, but at the home of Joaquin Slaza, the Dominican Consul in New York.

Rubi wore the same smoking jacket to his wedding with Hutton that he had worn to his wedding with Duke. Barbara wore a black dress and carried a scotch and soda down the aisle with her. The marriage contract was read in Spanish, as Hutton gently took Rubi's hand.

After the wedding, the bride and groom chartered a luxurious 86-seat jet for just the two of them and flew to Palm Beach for their honeymoon,

Married only two days, Barbara appeared from the honeymoon suite in front of friends with a broken ankle and because of his growing reputation, everyone thought it was the result of a fight with Rubi. (Nothing was ever proven.)

Once again, Rubi's "success" at the altar impressed the boss. During the honeymoon, Rubi received a reinstatement to the diplomatic corps as Minister Counselor in Paris from Trujillo, as well as being notified that he'd been named the best dressed man in America, an honor bestowed by famous designers from around the world.

It turned out that Trujillo himself was the one responsible for Barbara's sudden citizenship.

Increasingly, Hutton remained in her bedroom, now not only from illness, but also because of her ankle. Rubi wasn't a stay-at-home kind of guy and he soon disappeared for days at a time.

FBI memo dated 08/19/54 and classified "Secret," as were all such documents, read:

"Note on yellow. Attached reports reflect little information indicating positive anti-American sentiments, or as far as that is concerned, strong pro-American sentiments, on the part of Mrs. Rubirosa (Barbara Hutton) or of any of her husband's associates. But almost without exception her associates are described as members of the 'international set' characterized more specifically as pimps, homosexuals, gigolos, 'kept men of wealthy women,' or fortune hunters. Neither she nor they seem to be influenced by a strong sense of loyalty to the United States or any other country. Nationality to them appears to be a matter of opportunist expediency, or of limiting tax liability.

"Dissemination of all investigative reports is being made to the Department (FBI) at this time in view of the Department's expressed interest in the Rubirosas. Copies are being furnished to the INS and State Department because of the alien status of the Rubirosas and their associates described in the attached reports. It is also noted that Rubirosa has periodically held diplomatic status.

"Miss Hutton's attorney advised that she is a 'nice girl' but isn't too smart."

End of FBI document.

Strangely, his absence did not dampen Barbara's desire to continue showering him with gifts. She'd already given him the plantation in the Dominican, which was larger than Trujillo's, the ponies, and a sports car; now it was a room full of custom-made suits and 20 pairs of Italian shoes, along with a check for $2.5 million. Nevertheless, on the eve of his 45th birthday, the month following their marriage, she asked Rubi what he wanted. Her last word was barely off her lips when

he replied nonchalantly, "Why, my dear, I think I would like an airplane."

Within days, the grand airplane—another converted B-25 bomber—was ordered at a cost of $200,000, and along with it a bank account containing $50,000 to cover expenses for the plane.

Press accounts continued to be acerbic, when finally the subject of the two surfaced on television. Bob Hope was the first personality to use the Rubirosa marriage as fodder for comedy skits. He cracked, "Well, spring must be near. Barbara Hutton is getting ready to do her annual housecleaning."

Rubi and his B-25
Publicity was part of his job.
He was the DR's best PR.

A guest, George Jessel, wearing an eye patch a la Zsa Zsa, also did a bit on Barbara, spewing out a tired medley of one-liners:

"Barbara gets married so often, she only buys Minute Rice. But she's smart, she buys it by the case."

By far, the most strident evocation was sounded by the comedian Eddie Cantor. The last scene of one of Cantor's television scripts had the comedian in a black wig, impersonating Rubirosa on his wedding night, trying to force his way into his bride's bedroom, which is guarded in the scene by a pair of Pinkerton guards.

"The groom laments his bad fortune and decides to 'curl up with a good book,' at which point he produces three or four bankbooks. After some more charading and jokes, he says to the audience, 'My wife may be sleeping in there, but the best part of her is out here.' He holds up the bankbooks as the scene fades." (Source: *Poor Little Rich Girl*)

Not two weeks into the marriage, Rubi was bored. The growing monotony, coupled with his inability to forget his Hungarian love, resulted in another runaway from home. Rubi flew to Phoenix in his B-25 to see Zsa Zsa, and Hutton moved into her aunt Marjorie Merriweather Post's house in Palm Beach.

Among the many famous names Rubi romanced during that time was the sultry jazz singer, Eartha Kitt. In her autobiography *I'm Still Here: Confessions of a Sex Kitten*, she wrote, "There were a lot of jazz musicians and American artists in Paris at the time. I was introduced to him at the Chez Inez. The show went on with more and more important personalities coming backstage to meet Miss Dunham, one of them being Rubirosa.

"All the girls snickered and peeked around the theatre walls and curtains when we heard *he* was there. Handsome? God, he was handsome! The newspapers in Paris were full of news about Rubirosa and Barbara Hutton at the time....

"...I was standing by the side of the stage one night when

he was being ushered to Miss Dunham's dressing room suite. There were several men with him. I squeezed myself against the wall, giving him and his group more room to pass. He looked at me with a slight smile, making me cringe in embarrassment.

"I never had the slightest idea he would actually take me out on the town until a note came to my dressing room some days later, saying, 'I will pick you up tomorrow night after the show for dinner at Maxim's,' signed Rubirosa....

"...I can't go out with anyone like that, I said, wanting desperately to go. I don't have anything to wear. Besides, he and Maxim's are too fancy for me. At the same time, I thought, this might all be a joke. Why me?

"I slept very uneasily that night, half hoping that it was not a joke and half hoping it was. The phone rang the next morning: 'I am calling on behalf of Mr. Rubirosa,' the male voice said. 'He is confirming his request for dinner at Maxim's tonight. Will that be all right?'

"My brain went like a machine. How can this be? How did he get my phone number? How did he know what hotel? My mind ran faster and faster.

"...Oh...uh...I have nothing to wear, I called out. 'No matter, Mr. Rubirosa has

Eartha Kitt
Caught Rubi's eye

given me instructions to take you wherever you want to go shopping for anything you want—at his expense, of course.'

"...On our entrance into Maxim's, the violin quartet sere-naded us to a table with orchids, Dom Perignon champagne, and Beluga caviar displayed on ice. To me, this was a dream, a Hollywood I had missed when in Hollywood. Rubirosa was Cary Grant, Errol Flynn, Charles Boyer, Burt Lancaster, and Tyrone Power all in one, and I was out on the town with all of them."

X

After just 53 days, the marriage to Hutton was over.

On February 20, 1954, Rubi and Barbara were divorced. He immediately called a press conference to explain the divorce, saying, "I don't think Barbara is a sick woman, but for some reason she doesn't want to lead an active life. She would rather spend the entire day in bed and I came to realize that the marriage must end. I'm a healthy 45-year-old. My day starts early when I leap out of bed to a Spartan breakfast and head for polo practice.

"It scares be to think that someone like Barbara can while away a day in bed. I sincerely hoped that my wife could have changed her lifestyle."

In *Poor Little Rich Girl,* Sylvia Gable, a journalist, offered the only public rejoinder to Rubi's unflattering remarks:

"Rubi talks about a typical day! That's a laugh. Why, his typical day starts at 11 p.m. in the evening when he rolls out of bed and heads for the nearest nightclub. Surely, he knew that Barbara (Hutton) wasn't in perfect health when he mar-ried her. Shouldn't a husband show some compassion for the frailty of his wife?"

All told, the relationship cost Barbara more than $66,000 a day.

Some said that marked the end of Rubi's career as a pro-fessional stud (nevertheless, he would go on to marry once again), while establishing a record for stud fees. In the seven-and-a-half weeks they'd been together, he collected approximately $1 million in gifts, including the plantation, car, clothes, etc., and nearly $3 million in cash.

At first, Rubi returned to New York, checking in at the Plaza Hotel. However, as soon as the press reported his arrival, the phone began ringing. Throngs of women wanted to meet this 20th century playboy and furious husbands began calling as well, threatening to kill him for cavorting with their wives on the phone.

In a fit of aggravation, Rubi declared:

I am no different than a thousand other men who have fallen in love and married. For some reason, however, I am a monstrosity because I made the "mistake" of marrying a wealthy woman.

Now, I'm a freak, a cad. Women I've never met swear that I've called them long distance and made love to them over the phone, showing off to their husbands that at least someone loves them. I feel sorry for all of them who lead such shallow lives.

Hah, the great Rubirosa has made love to me far better than you—and that was over the phone. Imagine how he could make me feel in person," I could hear them yelling to their pitiful mates.

They can all go to hell as far as I'm concerned. I've done nothing. I merely pursue my passions and a joy for life. They could all do far worse.

Several days later, Rubi checked into the Jokake Inn Hotel in Los Angeles where Zsa Zsa had a friend reserve a room for him under the name of Cornelius Vandervault Whitney. The two rendezvoused that evening and Zsa Zsa later declared that it was just like before.

The following day, the couple secreted away to a friend of Zsa Zsa's home where they lazed the day away sunbathing, while oblivious to what was happening back at the hotel.

Rumors had spread that Rubirosa was back in town and journalists descended on the hotel. Still unaware, Rubi, Zsa Zsa, and her friend came back to the hotel at nightfall, coming through a back gate and down a narrow path lined with bushes.

Zsa Zsa and her friend were coming closer to the back entrance of the hotel, and Rubi followed several yards behind them. Suddenly, a reporter jumped out of the bushes and asked, "Is it true? Is Rubirosa back in town?"

Zsa Zsa formed an incredulous expression and answered, "How dare you!"

As the reporter was busy taking notes, Rubi had time to dive into the bushes to hide, an amusing scene—the famous Dominican Minister Plenipotentiary hiding in the bushes like a common thief.

Dismissing the reporter, Zsa Zsa and her friend went into the hotel and proceeded to hatch a plan to spirit Rubi away to a cabin in the mountains.

Following the tryst, the very public couple made a beeline to Paris, where they became mainstays on the international party circuit for the next year-and-a-half. The entertainment included spas, nightclubs, casinos, racetracks, and the ever-present polo ponies.

By late 1955, before they approached their final days together, and in order to help distract Rubi from his continued fits of jealousy, Zsa Zsa presented the idea to Republic Pictures for the two of them to do a movie together.

The script was called "Western Affair," written by Sundy Salt. It was an old western about the longstanding conflict between two rivals in love. Rubi was to play the role of Don Castillo, an elegant and shrewd saloonkeeper, and Zsa Zsa would play a French girl who had inherited an old saloon in Deadwood Gulch.

Eventually, she would get involved in a fight with Don Castillo, the "other" saloonkeeper in town. Their rivalry would soon turn into a passionate romance, resulting in the two bars joining.

Rubi was ecstatic. He signed a contract with Republic Pictures, which established the percentage of profits he would receive. In the film, he would be doing everything he loved: riding horses, boxing, shooting, and making love.

For the first time since he'd been in his early twenties, Rubi cleaned up his act. He stopped drinking, refrained from parties, and began to take drama lessons from a top teacher in Hollywood.

In the afternoon, Rubi would practice his fast-draw technique and at nights he would join with Gary Cooper, James Mason, and Humphrey Bogart to talk acting.

Just as filming was set to begin at Republic, the Immigration Department denied him permission to work, stating that since he was not a professional actor in his own country, he could not work as one in the United States.

Rubi was beyond furious. Still fuming, he returned to Paris where he expressed for some time, his annoyance with the way Zsa Zsa's adopted country had treated him. He began drowning his sorrows at bars.

By early 1956, the two had run out of steam. Zsa Zsa returned to Hollywood, married a succession of wealthy businessmen, and "revitalized" her sagging career around a series of late night television guest show appearances from which she profited handsomely.

Oddly, however, on one appearance on the Jack Parr show, she spoke of her love of polo ponies and jewelry, and purposely never mentioned Rubi.

✗

Later that year Rubi would be implicated once again by the FBI, in another murder, similar to the Morales assassination in 1935 in New York when his cousin was indicted.

According to **FBI documents,** "The District Attorney first had tried to see Rubirosa in 1956, soon after Dr. Jesus de Galindez, a Trujillo antagonist who was living in New York and teaching at Columbia University, disappeared under mysterious circumstances.

"Authorities believe de Galindez was kidnapped by Dominicans and taken back to the island, where he was killed. At the time of his disappearance, it was learned that Rubirosa had been in New York just before the murder of Bencosme (another anti-Trujillo exile from 1935) and left the day after that murder.

At this point, there isn't much information available as to what 'other' duties Rubi performed as Trujillo's confidant and in his various other diplomatic roles.

However, his relationship to Frank Sinatra, John F. Kennedy, and his connection to mobster Sam Giancana several years later would begin to connect many dots.

The fifth and last Mrs. Rubirosa
Rubi was finally tamed by a teenager.

7 Rubi Marries For Love

What sets Rubi apart from other men is that he gives the women, or the woman that he has chosen, whether that is for a night, a year, or forever, the impression that she is the center of the universe.

—Odile Rodin

At the age of 47, Porfirio Rubirosa's stamina and ardor were far from fading. Free from Gabor and divorced from Hutton, he was actually at the peak of his emotional and physical prowess. He renewed his career as the greatest playboy of all times, having affairs with Empress Soraya, Ava Gardener (the love of Frank Sinatra's life), and Rita Hayworth, among many others.

There has been considerable conjecture as to what Rubi's secret was with women. Some people claimed it was the daily dose of Japanese mushroom tea. However, he always denied that, saying he didn't need mushrooms to stay in shape.

Another version cited "pego palo," a substance from a Dominican tree, as the magic elixir. Rubi said that that claim was merely a marketing gimmick for the sale of the product as a love potion.

The press hounded me after my divorce from Barbara. The American magazine, Confidential, *ran a two-page photograph of me having a drink. It was just a Martini, but the caption read, "Here is Porfirio Rubirosa drinking a pega palo, the drink to which he owes his virility. He drinks a pega palo every day. Apparently, it contains certain roots found only in the Dominican forests. Pega palo is used to make infusions used as aphrodisiacs."*

After that article, I received hundreds of letters from tired men and disillusioned women. Everyone wanted me to urgently provide them with the elixir. A Texas firm even went to the Dominican Republic to obtain a supply. They paid a million dollars for it. What fools!

Dr. Soba, the Minister of Health in the Dominican, had been using my name without my permission to sell the roots, but when I confronted him, he said it was Trujillo giving the orders.

Rubi's closest friends were convinced his success was due, at least in part, to his captivating personality. Some men are just born with a special charisma that often puzzles them. Whatever the truth, perhaps some or all of it made Rubi a legend and a myth in his own time.

This was said of one of his protégés, the actor, George Hamilton, in a 1991 *Vanity Fair* article:

"Hamilton admitted that he hadn't helped his image much when Hollywood publicist Warren Cowan asked him who he saw himself as and he answered, Porfirio Rubirosa, the famous fifties playboy-diplomat who married Doris Duke and Barbara Hutton, and the daughter of the Dominican dictator, Trujillo."

✗

In Paris, in 1956, Rubi met a beautiful aspiring actress at a polo match in Deauville. She was 17-year-old Odile Rodin, and she had just been featured on the cover of *Paris Match* magazine.

Rubi later wrote, "I fell in love with her the first moment I saw her. She was young, fresh, so beautiful and, again, had a certain mysteriousness."

She had no idea who he was, nor of his notoriety, when she mentioned the encounter to her mother, who was a schoolteacher.

"You are forbidden to go around him. He is dangerous," her mother told her.

Mother Rodin's storm warnings soon dissolved into a puddle of affection after an evening out with her daughter and Rubi, when he asked her to dance first.

That summer Odile was staying on the Riviera, a guest of a wealthy industrialist, Paul Louis Weiller. One evening she took Weiller's Rolls Royce into Saint-Tropez to meet a friend for drinks. The friend announced that she had just motored over by boat and was staying with Rubi in Saint Jean Cap Ferrat with the Dubonnet's (the wine kings).

That was all Odile needed. She sent the driver and the Rolls back to Weiller and promptly jumped into a Chris Craft boat for the ride to Cap Ferrat. The choppy waters left her completely drenched and since she was only wearing a bikini top and thin white shorts, her appearance didn't leave much to the imagination when she stepped out of the boat and subsequently arrived at the Dubonnet's.

"When we got to the house, I made quite an entrance in my clingy, nearly see-through outfit and strappy sandals. I must have looked like a small Ursula Andress. Rubi was thrilled and the first thing he did was call Weiller to say that I wouldn't be home for dinner. Three days later, the Dubonnets sent their own Rolls to the Weillers to pick up the rest of my clothes," reported Rodin.

Thirty-one years separated the two, but Rubi and Odile were happy, perhaps because he had finally found someone who truly loved him. Rubi immediately began to play Pygmalion to his young bride's Galatea, demanding that she dress conservatively and in an understated manner. She was an aspiring actress who had come from a modest family and knew little about dressing elegantly, let alone acting the part.

For his part, Rubi wanted to turn her into the "Grande

dame," albeit a young one, devoting a considerable amount of time to teaching her elegant manners, how to dress, and how to walk.

Rubi wanted Odile to be the opposite of Zsa Zsa. If her hair was too lacquered or bizarre, he would pull her into the shower and rinse it out. He introduced her to couture, including Chanel and Balenciaga, wanting her to express her beauty and sexiness more like a Grace Kelly.

Odile would get even by going around without any underwear, no matter what she was wearing.

Odile describes Rubirosa:

"What sets Rubi apart from other men is that he gives the women, or the woman that he has chosen, whether that is for a night, a year, or forever, the impression that she is the center of the universe.

"I knew of him through what the newspapers had written and what people whispered about him in Paris. However, the moment he cornered me, I only thought about the warmth that he gave off and the sincerity of his feelings.

"When he would speak about the charms and beauty of his country, my only thought was that he had already played that card with other women. At the same time, I couldn't resist. Deep down, I thought he had to be right and months later, Rubirosa dragged me off to discover Santo Domingo.

"It was in June. The first night, we dined at a café. The next day, Rubi invited me to go dancing at the White Elephant and at Jimmy's. At that time, he was only a nice friend. Then vacation time came around and I took off to meet up with him on the Cote de Azure. It was then that he really began to reveal himself: very attentive, always happy from the moment he arises. He was capable of going out 10 nights in a row, but also seemingly just as happy to stay home with me and read or just watch television.

"One of the things that struck me about Rubi was that he

was never content to just go on a date with a woman. He always wants to get to know them deeper. He begins subtlety; perhaps by advising them on their makeup and hairstyle, not only to let them know he's paying attention, but to really advise them. He hates heavy makeup, especially lipstick and red fingernails.

"He would advise me about my hairstyle (he loved it up in a bun). He'd also consult me about my jewelry and tell me what he thought I should wear (he likes it simple). Regarding my dresses, he pays great attention to them. From the beginning of our relationship, I haven't purchased a single garment without him accompanying me to the design houses to advise and sometimes even impose his judgment on me.

"When Rubi's sister became very ill, we had to cut our vacation short and he left quickly for Santo Domingo. It was a melancholic separation. I was very much in love with him and I think he was with me as well.

Rubi and Odile
He wanted a
'Grande Dame'

"Almost from the minute he arrived back in Santo Domingo, he began phoning me, writing, and sending telegrams as long as novels.

"The night before he returned, I received a cablegram, which read, "I have something very important to tell you. Come and wait for me at my house."

"When he arrived home, he called again. I was filled with anticipation of what he would say to me.

"'What is that important thing, Rubi?'" I asked him immediately.

"'I can't live without you,'" he simply said.

"'And I cannot live without you,'" I replied

"'Then, Odile, we must get married.'"

"'If you wish.'"

"We left that night for my parents' house in Tournon. I come from a middle-class family, however; it is filled with professors of medicine. The idea of seeing their daughter married to a character like Porfirio Rubirosa did not make the Bernards happy. My mother had already forewarned me on many occasions.

"'Do you know what you're getting into?'" she asked.

"'Yes, Mother.'"

"'Don't say I didn't warn you,'" she replied.

"I was rehearsing at the theater every day. As the rehearsals became increasingly difficult, I became increasingly nervous, to the point that on opening night, I was a trembling wreck, even a bit terrified, and I sensed that Rubi was nearly as nervous for me.

"In spite of our apprehensions, everything went well. The play, by Marcel Pagnol, was well-received and got good reviews. The big magazines started to become interested in me and I began to get movie offers. I would have loved to promote my career, but success was not as tempting as spending my time with Rubi.

"We married on the 27th of October in Gonchamps, at the home of our friends, Bernard and Nicole Boge. No invitations were sent and only a handful of close friends attended.

"That same evening, I still had to act and I went to the theater, but my heart wasn't in it. The discipline that the play imposed upon me was quite tiresome. During those first few months, I would have much preferred to have dedicated my time to making love with Rubi, so I started to find ways out.

I began by faking a cold so I could have a weekend with my love in London. An understudy replaced me adequately, so I felt no guilt.

"While in London that weekend, Rubi and I were dancing at the Ambassador's Club, where we unfortunately ran into my manager, Adres Bernheim.

"'So, this is your cold?'" he said, somewhat surprised.

"He was not happy, which I understood. He did not understand that the state of mind of an actress is not compatible with the mind of a newlywed.

"In the end, I rescinded my contract and Rubi and I went on a honeymoon to Santo Domingo, one of the most beautiful countries I'd ever seen. Rubi did all the cooking and I studied my Spanish, and we made love incessantly."

Later, in 1958, President Trujillo named Rubi Ambassador to Cuba. Fidel Castro, who would come to power in a year, was fascinated with Rubi. The two spent hours talking about how Trujillo stayed in power in the Dominican Republic for so long.

Odile would remark that at the age of 19, she was the youngest "ambassadress" in the world.

Meanwhile, Rubi was introducing his ex-brother-in-law to his Hollywood society friends.

President Trujillo had sent his son to study at the war college in Ft. Leavenworth, Kansas, and Ramfis arrived in full splendor, anchoring his father's yacht at Frisco Bay, Texas, complete with his own musicians.

In early 1958, Rubi introduced Ramfis to Zsa Zsa who in turn hosted a candlelight dinner for fellow actress, Kim Novak.

The spark between the two was evident that first night, but Zsa Zsa, playing matchmaker, left nothing to chance. She staged a lavish party to honor friends, David Selznik, Jennifer Jones, Shirley Maclaine, Robert Mitchum, Natalie Wood, and

Ramfis and Kim Novak
Chinchilla warmed up
the Masarati

others—and, of course, Ramfis.

Rubi arrived, Odile in arm, and was immediately given a large bear hug by Ramfis, who said, "My brother, I adore you for introducing me to Zsa Zsa. Because of her, I am in love with Kim. I can scarcely contain myself."

I was happy for Ramfis and proud of Zsa Zsa. Despite our differences in the past, she was quite cordial and kind to Odile as well. The party was a huge success and then the Dom flowed into the wee hours. I was certainly not enamored of the Hollywood types. However, I must admit, there were more gorgeous starlets in that room than I'd ever seen in one place before, even in Paris.

I could feel Odile's eyes on my neck all night and I took particular pains not to indulge my baser desires.

Eventually, Ramfis blamed his relationship with Kim Novak, for his inability to finish his studies. In the interim, however, he showered both Zsa Zsa and Novak with extravagant gifts. For Zsa Zsa, there was a red Mercedes with a chinchilla coat in the trunk, among other things.

Ramfis presented the car to Zsa Zsa one evening, while she was rehearsing for the George Gobel Show in Burbank. The car, a rare model, had been flown to Burbank from Kansas. The bright red two-seater was sitting on Hollywood

Boulevard wrapped in an enormous ribbon—red, of course. On the driver's side, there was a card attached to the door handle—a thank you note for introducing him to Kim.

Kim received an $8,500 Masarati, in a matching red as well.

Zsa Zsa explained that the car (a convertible) came first and she was so cold driving it with the top down, the chinchilla coat was a logical second gift.

The exorbitant price of these gifts prompted an outraged congressman in Washington to say, "It is absurd to offer financial assistance to a nation in which the President's son is squandering money on presents to glamorous movie stars."

When it was revealed that the U.S. was giving the Dominican Republic $1,300,000 in economic aid, there was talk of a Congressional Investigation and the army school subsequently refused to give Ramfis his diploma.

Later that year (1958), Ramfis announced he was divorcing his wife, with whom he'd fathered six children, and then he promptly asked Kim's mother for her hand in marriage.

A month later, Zsa Zsa and Kim were guests at a reception hosted by Ramfis on his father's yacht, the *Angelita,* which was stocked with almost as many Dominican soldiers as bottles of champagne.

The following evening, Ramfis moved the yacht to Santa Monica Harbor to be closer to Zsa Zsa and Kim's homes.

At the time, the *Angelita* was the largest, most luxurious and expensive private yacht in the world. (Originally, it was commissioned by financier, E.F. Hutton, Barbara's uncle.)

When the yacht was subsequently moved to Long Beach, the actress Joan Collins became a frequent guest.

Later that year, Ramfis met his soon-to-be second wife, actress Lita Milan, while partying with Zsa Zsa, Rubi, and Novak at the Mocambo nightclub.

Rubirosa made it a point
to know all the right people.

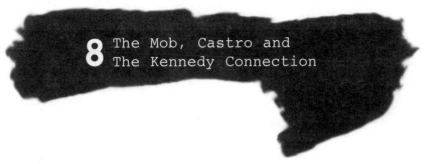

What do we have on Rubirosa?

—J. Edgar Hoover,
Former Director, FBI

During the '50s, before Castro took over, Cuba, just 95 miles from the Dominican Republic, was a gambling Mecca controlled by the mafia, or more precisely, the Chicago mob.

In 1952, when Batista, a former army stenographer, seized power, Cuba was known as the Paris of the New World. While the Havana nightlife might have been like Paris, the gentle breezes, balmy days, and piercing cobalt blue Caribbean waters were more reminiscent of the French Riviera that Rubi knew so well.

Europeans and Americans came in droves to lie on powdery beaches under gently swaying palm trees during the day and to dance the nights away. Many listened to the brassy voice of jazz singer Eartha Kitt as they gulped daiquiris and smoked foot-long cigars, and then adjourned to the casinos where thousands were left on the tables in a nightly ritual.

When American tourists reached Havana after a 5-hour flight from New York, they had a choice of five or six swank hotels, including gangster Meyer Lansky's Montmarte Club or his elegant Hotel Nacional, which overlooked El Morro, the ancient fortress protecting Havana's harbor.

Havana had a claim to being the world's premier play city, swaying to the rhythms of the rumbas, sambas, and mambos, which it had exported to Europe and America through count-less white tuxedoed orchestras, all of which Rubi was well accustomed to—he'd practically been raised on the sounds in Paris.

Celebrities like Ernest Hemingway, actor George Raft, Marilyn Monroe, and many others could be seen sitting at dark tables under clouds of cigar smoke, or being chauffeured around Havana in American luxury cars; and, of course, thanks to Meyer Lansky and the mob, gambling was the other draw. In fact, it was a time of complete abandon and a free-for-all without any regulations—the mob and many unsavory Cuban nightclub owners were running casinos in nearly every club.

Some were run by serious, professional operators, but most had little experience—just a bankroll. There were a lot of quick returns on minimal investments thanks to "come on" games like a version of three-card-Monte and many others.

Soon, stories began to cir-culate that the wealthy American tourists were being fleeced, roundly.

Batista saw the enhancement of revenues from foreign visitors, Americans in particular, as a major source of future income for the island—and for himself—and, so, he was the first to begin to clean up the clubs.

With the development of hotel chains and airlines in the 1950s, tourism was just starting to be seen as an "industry."

Fidel Castro and Rubi talked politics for hours

Cuba's climate, beaches, and proximity to New York and Miami, and the beauty of their women, were all undeveloped assets. At the time, the same was true for the Dominican Republic, which would soon be on the mob's list as potential tourism sites.

In 1953, Fidel Castro first arrived on everyone's radar, including that of the U.S. On July 26, he led a revolt in which 100 men and women attacked the Moncado army barracks, near Santiago de Cuba. The attack was a failure and Castro was arrested. Most of his men were killed or imprisoned. Castro went on trial and on October 16, he was sentenced to 15 years in prison.

After Batista's cleanup, Cuban gaming opened up in the 1954-55 season in a reformed state. Gone were most of the crooked games replaced by blackjack and other more traditional Vegas-style games. Even the American embassy closed their books on the allegations and substantiations of cheating.

Meyer Lansky's Montmarte Club remained the premier destination for high rollers—serious gambling for serious players. Not far from there stood the Nacional, a hotel that bore a striking resemblance to the Breakers in Palm Beach. Lansky was hatching a scheme to take over a wing of the hotel and refurbish it with luxury suites for his high-stakes players.

The Americans, who frequented the Nacional as a sort of expatriate club, did not take kindly to that idea. They did not want things to change.

Though the Cuban government owned the Nacional, Batista saw it as the chance to show off his dynamic new tourist policy. In 1955, the Nacional was placed under "new management."

The American singer Eartha Kitt became the star of the new floorshow, and the new casino opened in 1955, proving to be a huge success.

[*Sidebar:* In 1956, Fidel Castro and his revolutionaries were released early from prison in a general amnesty.]

By 1956, Lansky owned and operated three hotels, and he and Batista were, essentially, partners.

By late 1956, Havana had attracted many of America's professional gamblers. Most of the major Vegas players were there as well.

Lansky's dreams had come true. He could never have obtained a gaming license or operated openly in Las Vegas, but now, practically earshot from Miami, he was running a wide-open operation in a legal setting that was, in many ways, more agreeable than the remote Nevada desert. Soon, his empire was being called the Havana Riviera.

During the 1957-58 season, Havana offered visitors a rare and extravagant experience. The gaming in the casinos was very different from just three years earlier. It was now a hushed, almost reverent setting, befitting the seriousness of the stakes. Even a strict dress code was enforced. Many men wore tuxedos and the women wore serious jewelry.

Compared to the raucous carnival atmosphere outside, the Montmarte and others, were asylums of gentility.

The revolution had begun. After Castro's release from prison, he joined Che Guevara in Mexico and began to train troops. Batista's army was unprepared for the fighting conditions and the guerilla style of warfare. His troops deserted or surrendered, en masse. Eventually, he decided the situation was hopeless.

No one could have predicted the astounding turn of events

within just that year. Early in 1958, Batista sent his children's passports to the American embassy to be stamped with U.S. visas. On December 9, President Eisenhower dispatched a personal emissary to Batista, promising unhindered access to and asylum in the dictator's Daytona Beach home, provided Batista would leave Cuba quickly. Within a week, the "stenographer dictator" had picked up his winnings, put his family in planes at the neighboring air force base, and fled the country, eventually winding up in Spain with $300,000,000.

With the country in a state of war/anarchy, it looked like Rubi's ambassadorship was on the line when a bomb was thrown in the backyard of the Dominican embassy while Rubi and Odile were away at lunch.

Returning to the embassy, they found Dominican soldiers scurrying about in preparation for an attack. A soldier with an automatic weapon was standing post at each of the corner gates, sights trained on the unruly crowds gathering and growing by the hour.

It wasn't just the Dominican embassy that had been attacked. The revolutionaries' zeal stoked the fires of emotion within everyone. There seemed to be no sides taken, just destruction and chaos; many buildings were on fire and the constant crack of rifle shots rang in Rubi's ears.

Odile was in tears as plumes of smoke rose around the compound walls and began to burn everyone's eyes. Batista forces were lobbing tear gas canisters into the violent crowd.

Rubi ran through the embassy rooms gathering up some of Odile's things and then they locked themselves into a basement room to wait for dark and an escape.

Seemingly overnight, Castro was in power.

Under cover of dark, with random gunshots piercing the night air, Rubi and Odile jumped into a Dominican embassy jeep and drove immediately to the home of the American ambassador, Earl Smith, and his wife, Flo. Odile recalled that the machinegun fire was incessant and that it seemed the world was coming apart at the seams. What seemed to trouble Rubi the most, however, was getting his polo ponies out of the country.

[*Sidebar:* Fidel Castro had taken the first step to destroy the traditional legal system that had governed Cuba since independence. Thereafter, laws would be what the country's Maximum Leader said they were.

[While Castro gave his support to freedom of the press, while traveling in the United States, a revolutionary court in Havana sentenced a columnist to ten years at hard labor for writing that the rebels were a bunch of "thieves and bandits." Castro stated that he thought that the words of Lincoln supported the ideals of the Cuban revolution.]

On May 7, Castro returned to Havana and was met at the airport by Philip Bonsal, the American ambassador, who asked for an early meeting to discuss relations between the two countries. Castro readily agreed. The same day the cabinet voted to suspend the rights of habeas corpus in Cuba for a period of ninety days.

Seeing that Cuba no longer had anything to offer the Dominican Republic, Trujillo offered Rubi a choice of new posts, either Belgium or Argentina. Rubi chose the latter, not only because Odile had family there, but also because the country was famous for polo.

Trujillo was facing his own problems at home when out of the blue, he forced Rubi to trade his coffee plantation to him for stocks—an "investment" that was soon worthless. The president needed the money, as his political base was crumbling and his life was now in constant danger.

The 1959 revolution or coup brought all of the fun and decadence to a screeching halt as Fidel Castro's communist regime moved rapidly to close down the casinos and choke off the mob, which just as quickly started looking for another idyllic island on which to conduct business—one also preferably close to the U.S. mainland.

The parameters of the search were simple: Find a small, poor island run by a corrupt dictator who would allow the mob to build casinos and hide, or launder, its ill-gotten gains in phony banks. There would also have to be powdery beaches, balmy breezes, and a lush inviting landscape.

Central America was immediately dismissed, even though most of those countries were virtually run by the CIA and the mob. It was *too* hot, underdeveloped, and *too* poor. After all, paying tourists in search of a good time don't want to look at sweaty, poor people, in miserable conditions.

After a considerable amount of due diligence, the mob decided upon the Dominican Republic, just 500 miles from Florida and close to Cuba—the perfect fit in every way but one—the dictator, Rafael Trujillo, was beginning to warm up to the Soviet bloc and if that happened, the U.S. would certainly pull its support from the island. Besides, Trujillo was also losing his mind. (Source: Americanmafia.com 2001)

When Cuba fell, it also inspired the anti-Trujilloistas (left wing Dominicans who were now seeking help from the revolutionary government of Cuba).

The first organized uprising occurred when exiled Dominicans flew 14 seaplanes into the Dominican Republic in June, in the hopes of ousting Trujillo. Called The Luperion Invasions, it was quickly crushed by Trujillo's army and air force and the survivors were rounded up and executed.

That was followed by small groups of young Dominicans forming underground organizations dedicated to overthrowing the Trujillo regime.

However, Trujillo's real concerns were with Venezuela's President Romulo Betancourt, who was an established and outspoken opponent of Trujillo and who had been associated with some of the individual Dominicans who were plotting against Trujillo.

Trujillo developed an obsessive personal hatred of Betancourt and supported numerous plots of Venezuelan exiles to overthrow him, which led to the Venezuelan government taking its case against Trujillo to the Organization of American States (OAS). This, of course, infuriated Trujillo, who ordered his agents to assassinate Betancourt. In June of 1960, Betancourt was injured, but was not killed.

The entire incident inflamed world opinion against Trujillo and prompted the OAS to sever ties with the Dominican and impose sanctions against the country.

Prior to Kennedy, President Eisenhower had tolerated Trujillo as a bulwark of stability in the Caribbean and some still saw him as a desirable counterforce to the Castro regime. Public opinion in the U.S., however, began to run against the Dominican dictatorship.

Kennedy won the election in 1960 and immediately inherited the Caribbean situation along with the mob. Kennedy was not prepared to coexist with another Cuba, and the Dominican leader had become a political embarrassment to the U.S. hemispheric policy.

The Eisenhower administration had wanted to depose Trujillo and impose an American government, or at least one sympathetic, so an intervention policy was aggressively pursued with threats of military intervention, covert aid to Dominican dissidents, multilateral diplomacy, and political pressures through the OAS.

Throughout the 20th century, the U.S. objectives in the hemisphere had been to prevent the rise to power of any government that could threaten the security of the United States, particularly those as close as Cuba and the Dominican Republic.

The political character of Latin American regimes was irrelevant, if they maintained internal order and supported

U.S. policies. Of course, if the regime were more rightist, so much the better. The U.S. had just emerged from the communist witch-hunt era of Joseph McCarthy, so everyone was walking on eggshells around any potential leftist bent.

Kennedy's concern was that Trujillo was beginning to warm to the Soviets. For 30 years prior, however, Trujillo had adhered fervently to U.S. policies and desires, but in the '50s, as just mentioned, Trujillo's support was wearing thin.

The fear was that Trujillo's collapse would lead to chaos and the emergence of a second Castro in the Dominican. However, at the very same time, the mob was actively working with various elements within the Dominican, to satisfy their own agenda.

✗

Kennedy became president in January of 1961.

Kennedy's Secretary of State, Dean Rusk, agreed that the Dominican dictator had become a threat, but both continued to rely on overt OAS actions and covert CIA operations in the country, just as Eisenhower before him.

Enter the CIA-mob connection. The lucrative Cuban gaming industry had long since expired and the mob was still trying to gain a foothold in the Dominican.

The challenge for the mob would be to get the Kennedy administration to commit support, regardless of Trujillo's political affiliations. That's when they turned to Rubi, the legendary playboy/diplomat.

Though Rubi had spent most of his life to that point in such far flung locales as Paris, New York, and Palm Beach seducing rich socialites, driving in Le Mans races, or wearing out polo ponies, by that time he'd been an ambassador for the Republic for many years as well. He was the best PR Trujillo had. However, now, he was more engaged at home.

As such, he was responsible for ensuring that companies

doing business with Trujillo included an extra 15%—a special tax on their invoices, if you will—that would go to El Presidente.

Rubi was also in charge of keeping an eye on any American dissidents, usually with the help of mob contacts. It was said that he would then turn that information over to the Servicio Intelligencia Militar, or the secret police. (Source: American Mafia.com. Article 181)

During the spring of 1961, Rubi started spending time with Frank Sinatra, Peter Lawford, and Dean Martin.

His introduction to Giancana came because of a weekend spent on a luxury yacht off the French coast with Sinatra, Lawford, and Martin. It is suspected that Sinatra was acting as the conduit between Kennedy, the mob (Giancana), Rubirosa, and the elite within the Dominican Republic, which was plotting to overthrow Trujillo.

It is also reported that with a verbal commitment from Rubi and the Republic's elite, the mob would be free to operate there once Trujillo was gone. All that was needed were assurances that if the mob assisted in the Dominican Republic military replacing Trujillo, the new government would be pro-United States.

It appears Rubi, as usual, was straddling the fence in an effort to survive and to again thrive. Was he a triple threat? He appeared to be working with Trujillo's secret police *and* the mob, while at the same time, working with the Dominican's elite who wanted nothing more than to dispose of Trujillo and to chum up to Kennedy. Perhaps he was trying to cover all his bases in any eventuality.

Regardless of his agenda, the one thing that Rubi was loyal to was his country, not Trujillo. He loved his people and perhaps he was struggling with how best to serve them.

Certainly, his connection to Sinatra, Kennedy, and ultimately Giancana, indicated his desire to rid the country of the evil one.

All his life, he'd been the Generalissimo's "PR" man, but it's easy to see he may have seen himself as a puppet. Once he'd recognized just how evil Trujillo was (perhaps beginning with being undermined in the dredging incident by his ex-father-in-law and then culminating with the discovery of the genocide of the Haitians), he might have secretly wished for his demise, but no doubt, at least used that association to further his own lifestyle and connections.

It is also easy to surmise that once Trujillo was gone, the Dominican Republic

Sam Giancana
He had friends in high places

would again be on a good footing with the U.S. Rubi had cemented his own mob ties, and life could potentially be good again, so Rubi continued to play both sides of the fence.

Because of his meeting with Sinatra, Lawford, and Martin, Rubi was invited by Sinatra to meet with Kennedy on Cape Cod later in September of 1961. It may never be known exactly what Kennedy, Rubirosa, and Sinatra actually discussed out on the Cape that day, but a month later, Kennedy gave CIA Director Alan Dulles the okay to assassinate Trujillo and Sam Giancana began his plans to create another Cuba in the

Dominican Republic. Coincidence? (Source: American Mafia.com. Feature article 181.).

✗

From that point on, Rubi went through a succession of posts. First, as Ambassador to Belgium, but after a prolonged absence or even an appearance at the embassy, Trujillo canceled the appointment.

However, as he'd done several times before, it wasn't long before Trujillo reinstated Rubi, this time in June of 1961 as the appointed Inspector of Embassies and Legations. His duties would be to inspect all the Dominican embassies throughout the world. Everyone agreed there could be no better post for a man who had been a globetrotter all his life.

He could have traveled anywhere, but Rubi only visited five places—Deauville, California, Texas, Florida, and the Riviera—all better suited to tourists than to an inspector. Mostly, he acted like a tourist, not a diplomat.

Rubi's appeal to both men and women became very publicly apparent by his new and close relationship with Frank Sinatra.

Soon, Rubi became friends with the entire entourage (known as the Rat Pack), including Sammy Davis, Jr., who had this to say about Rubi:

"I spent three weeks in Paris and met Rubi, Frank's new best friend. Rubi was the most elegant man I had ever met. It's easy to understand why a president's daughter and wealthy heiresses married him....

"...He was enchanting, mysterious, surprising, and very attractive. Without a doubt the best dressed man in the world. The way Rubi dressed made me feel like I fell in a dumpster. I was very impressed to meet and know him.

"Rubi could read people's minds and deduce anything. He was naturally intuitive. He knew how to live among the

Rubi, Sinatra's new 'best friend,' was an honorary Rat Packer-Er

'nobility' and 'royalty.' I asked him how he did it and he said, 'I give them the respect they deserve because of who they are and then we become equals.'

"If I started the day with Rubi, we would be drinking Salty Dogs before lunch. We would drink all day and all night. But you never saw Rubi red-eyed or with bags under his eyes.

"How do you manage to dress so well?" I asked Rubi.

"'Your job is to be an entertainer. My job is to be a play-boy,' he answered.

"I asked him if he ever worked [had a job].

"'Work? There's no time for work.'

"I never heard Rubi say a bad or negative thing about any-one. He was just a great guy and a good friend."

The press hounded me about Sinatra—not Sammy, or Peter, or Dean, just Frank. I was often asked to help some reporter get an interview with him. On one occasion, a magazine where I had some friends asked me to get them an exclusive interview with Frank. They said they would only take a few pictures and would give Frank a preview of the text before publishing it. I doubted that Frank (Sinatra) would go for it, knowing all that he'd been through, but I asked him anyway. He emphatically declined. He said that when he'd been on the Riviera that same magazine had put a bug in his room. When Frank made up his mind, nothing could change it.

His private life was always a scandal, worse than mine. He was accused of doing the worst possible things. The press hounded him constantly and tried to report on the most intimate details of his private life. I felt an affinity for him. He was the most enchanting singer I had ever listened to.

FBI memos and files show that Rubi was spending most of his time in Palm Beach and New York bars, but he found time to make sure that companies doing business with Trujillo paid kickbacks to the dictator. As roving ambassador, or Inspector of Embassies, he was in charge of keeping track of any dissidents, those who would try to undermine Trujillo's feared secret police, the SIM. The FBI discovered, Rubi was a senior agent in that organization.

Rubi also accomplished responsibilities with the help of New York mobsters. In short, Rubi was the de facto leader of the Dominican's elite. With his help and a verbal commitment, the mob could eliminate Trujillo, clearing the way for the Kennedy administration to once again recognize the island, assuming any replacement would be pro-U.S. (Source: American Mafia.com)

According to an FBI document dated 03-21-61 (which has mostly blacked out certain names):

"(Unknown) has furnished the following information:

Porfirio Rubirosa, who has served as Dominican Ambassador to various European countries and currently occupies the position of Ambassador to France is an agent of the Dominican Military Intelligence Service (SIM)."

The document is blacked out for the next two paragraphs and then resumes, "(Unknown) advised the fact that (unknown), in his opinion, conclusively proves that he is a SIM Agent.

"This document contains neither recommendations nor conclusions of the FBI. It is the property of the FBI, and is loaned to your agency. It and its contents are not to be distributed outside your agency...knowledge of specific assignments given to Rubirosa nor could he furnish any information regarding Rubirosa's salary as a SIM Agent."

Other files obtained from the FBI indicate a flurry of activity between the FBI and the INS during 1961, the year that Rubi started spending more time with Sinatra and Kennedy. The FBI advised the INS on several occasions to, "Place appropriate stops in the event the subject (Rubirosa) entered the country and to ascertain if he was traveling on an official passport."

According to American Mafia.com, "Rubi was going to be in New York anyway. He'd been summoned by the New York District Attorney to be questioned about his role in the kidnap and torture of several Dominican exiles, probably as the result of the insistence of the FBI.

The day before the meeting in Cape Cod, Sinatra had spent the afternoon at the White House with performers Danny Kaye and Judy Garland, teaching them how to make Bloody Marys and then leisurely sipping them out on the rear balcony that overlooks the Washington Monument.

"The following day, Sinatra took the president's private plane to the Kennedy's summer home on the Cape, along with Ted Kennedy, Pat Lawford, and Odile. Upon arriving, the group went on a three-hour cruise on the president's yacht, The Honey Fitz.

Supposedly, the CIA had been contacting conservative Dominicans who opposed Trujillo. Agents made contact with once loyal Trujillistas, who were now plotting an assassination of the dictator.

The published account says that wealthy Dominicans who had personal vendettas against the dictator, or who had family members who had suffered at the hands of the SIM, were the co-conspirators. Some even included relatives of Trujillo.

The CIA, of course, did not want to appear to be involved, so it is suspected that mob figures, and perhaps Rubi, helped smuggle in the rifles used in the assassination.

New FBI wiretap records from 1961 confirm phone conversations between Rubirosa and Romanian arms dealer Jean Koree. As always, with Rubi anything is possible.

On May 30, 1961, five months after Kennedy took office, the conspirators assassinated Trujillo by firing into the dictator's car on a deserted patch of highway.

He was on his way to San Cristobal, accompanied only by his chauffeur. When they stopped at a lonely intersection, several men jumped from the bushes with automatic weapons and in a Bonnie and Clyde ending, the car and its two occupants were riddled with bullets, both dying instantly.

However, the full coup attempt failed (Trujillo was the only one killed). When the assassins went into hiding, Rubi's friend, and the dictator's son, Ramfis, assumed control of the Dominican Republic the next day, at least in a de facto sense.

When Rubi first met with Ramfis the day after the assassination, Ramfis asked Rubi to visit Kennedy in Washington.

"Ask President Kennedy, your friend, to have the Organization of American States lift the sanctions against us. It will be needed to restore lasting order."

On June 6, 1961, *The New York Journal American*, a daily newspaper published in New York City, ran an article captioned, "Trujillo Jr. Wants Free Nation, Not Power." It was written by Igor Cassini, who was a public relations man and who wrote a syndicated column called *Smart Set*.

Just three days later an internal **FBI document (97-1552)** commented on the article.

"The *Journal* article indicates that Porfirio Rubirosa has arrived in New York on a very important mission and refers to Rubirosa as a former ambassador to many countries who has cast off his playboy mantle, at least temporarily, and has assumed the role of diplomat.

"Cassini writes that it was in this 'serious' role that Rubirosa gave him an exclusive interview shortly after Rubirosa arrived at Idlewild Airport.

"According to the article, Rubirosa told Cassini that Rafael Trujillo, Jr., the head of the new Dominican Joint Chiefs of Staff, has no desire to continue the so-called 'Trujillo dynasty,' that he personally has no political ambitions, wants to resume as fast as possible, diplomatic relations with the United States and other Latin American countries, and scorns any 'under the table' arrangements with Soviet Russia.

"According to the article, Rubirosa pointed out that Trujillo, Jr., stands for free elections and that a general amnesty will be granted to all political prisoners and Dominican exiles.

"The remainder of the article is in question and answer form. To answer a question as to the purpose of his trip, Rubirosa said, 'I am here unofficially, you understand, but I came with the blessing of President Balaguer and General Trujillo (Jr.).'

"In his column, Cassini also indicates that Porfirio Rubirosa 'was notified today by telephone from Ciudad Trujillo that President Balaguer had appointed him roving ambassador at-large.'"

It is difficult to determine what the FBI knew about Rubi's subsequent stay in New York the following month, because those documents obtained by us have blacked out many of the names. They (FBI) were definitely interested in Rubi and they had his Gotham Hotel phone bugged for days.

FBI records indicate over 40 leads were investigated over Rubi's phone conversations and subsequent leads.

Records don't reveal who Rubi called from his room, but they do reveal phone calls to New York, the Dominican Republic, and Washington, D.C. (whose number it is noted was that of the Justice Department)—and a call to President Kennedy's private number in Cap Cod.

It is surmised that in this meeting, Rubi asked for intervention with the OAS, as Ramfis had requested. Kennedy's reply was that the Trujillo "family" establish a democratic government and return all properties to their rightful owners, or he could do nothing.

According to FBI document NY-97-2078, dated August 1961:

"(Name blacked out) advised he had received the following information from a Cuban who is residing in New York City and is familiar with the thinking of the majority of the Cuban and Dominican exiles in the New York area.

"This Cuban advised (name blacked out) that recent publicity given to the association between Peter Lawford, the brother-in-law of the President, and Porfirio Rubirosa, who was described by (name blacked out) as a long- time Trujillo henchman known to Latin American's as a lobbyist for the Trujillo family, has created an extremely bad impression among Cuban and Dominican exiles in the New York City area.

"(Name blacked out) explained that when Latin Americans saw a photograph of Lawford and Rubirosa together, they took it for granted that Rubirosa had access to President Kennedy through his brother-in-law."

Still further FBI memorandums clearly show that there was no love lost between Dominicans and President Kennedy. **Document NY 9-2078**:

"On November 10, 1961, (name blacked out) advised that he had been told that Porfirio Rubirosa, an individual who has served as Dominican Ambassador to various European countries, reportedly had been in recent contact with (name blacked out), whom described as (sentence blacked out) coup d'etat in the Dominican Republic.

"Rubirosa allegedly disclosed to (blacked out) that if economic and diplomatic sanctions against the Dominican Republic were not lifted or alleviated by November 10, 1961, there would be a coup d'etat in the Dominican. This coup presumably would be in accordance with the plan of (blacked out)."

However, that date was pushed back, as the rest of the FBI memo notes:

"On November 13, 1961, (blacked out) made available an article which appeared in the October 23, 1961 issue of the Dominican newspaper, "El Caribe." The article is a reproduction of an article that appeared in an American newspaper and according to (blacked out), it reflected that Rubirosa is a close associate of the family of President Kennedy. (Blacked out) stated that the Dominican press and radio undoubtedly give a great deal of publicity to this association, which gives the implication that the Kennedy administration is supporting General Rafael Trujillo, Jr. and the Joaquin Balaguer regime in the Dominican.

"(Blacked out) states that this is a very dangerous situation and in his opinion, the Dominican opposition will be increasingly inclined to take an anti-American stand if this type of publicity continues."

In yet another **FBI paper**, it is noted:

"The association of Rubirosa with President Kennedy has disappointed many Dominicans who dream of freedom. More and more of them have been listening to radio broadcasts of Fidel Castro from Cuba offering 35,000 Czech-made machineguns to support any revolt against the regime. He is trying to identify the Trujillo-Balaguer regime with the United States."

It is interesting to note that during these turbulent times in the Dominican Republic, which were both horrible and wonderful, it wasn't Ramfis Trujillo, nor Joaquin Balaguer, who were speaking for the country. Only one man was acting as spokesman—Porfirio Rubirosa.

After all his discussions with Kennedy, Rubi returned to the Dominican to report to Ramfis on his progress, or lack thereof. Ramfis' reply was, "If we do what Kennedy wants, we'll all be broke. However, there is one alternative, which may help both of us."

"What is that?" Rubi asked.

"I will place all of our holdings into shares of a trust. We'll call it Molinos Dominicanos. If you place your money in it, you will retire wealthy."

Rubi replied that he only had $500,000 left to his name, but Ramfis convinced him that he could increase that exponentially by investing in his trust.

Shortly thereafter, Ramfis fled the country for France with a boatload of money on his father's yacht, the *Angelita*, to the shock of Rubirosa who had deposited half a million dollars into Ramfis' account.

Flor de Oro estimated that her half-brother took more than $200 million out of the trust before he left the country, $500,000 of which belonged to Rubi.

Before fleeing, Ramfis, through informers, found his father's four assassins. They were all seated around a table in a rundown roadside bar, drinking and laughing, more than likely celebrating. Ramfis entered alone with a Thompson sub-machinegun, one of the many the CIA had shipped into the country.

Upon seeing him, the men jumped up, each with his hand on his holster, but they were not fast enough. Ramfis sprayed them and the bar with a full clip, then turned and shot two soldiers that had come in from outside.

That was the last time anyone in the Dominican Republic saw him in the country.

At that point, the new president, Joaquin Balaguer, terminated Rubi's job as roving ambassador, putting him out of work. Rubi begged Balaguer to appoint him as Minister of Tourism, but the new president refused, preferring to clean out all the old laundry; anything associated with Trujillo.

FBI documents, dated March 30, 1962, stated:

"Dominican government requests extradition of Ramfis Trujillo. This news item in *La Prensa*, a Spanish language daily newspaper in New York, reflected that the Dominican government had asked the French government for the extradition of Rafael Trujillo as well as that of the ex-diplomat, Porfirio Rubirosa.

"A foreign ministry spokesman informed that instructions had been sent to the Dominican Embassy in Paris so that it will see to it that those criminals be placed under arrest or at least, be forbidden to leave French territory."

According to a later article in *The London Sunday Express*, writer Susan Barnes recounted her conversation with Rubi upon his return to the Dominican after his meetings with Kennedy:

"I said to Ramfis, 'You must support the new president and give back the things your father stole from the people...but he didn't have the guts...and he was out. He took his yacht and went to Paris. I won't ever see him again in my life. He is not my friend. He betrayed me.'"

Barnes remembered the interview, not so much for Rubi's political comments as for what happened afterward. According to her, though it seems uncharacteristic of Rubi, as she went to the bathroom of his suite at the Hotel Savoy to freshen up, she encountered a "grinning" Rubirosa standing in his monogrammed boxer shorts, through which stood his "apparatus."

Rubi's relationship with the Kennedys alarmed the FBI

"He threw me onto his unmade bed and a wrestling match ensued as this grotesque thing swung about."

Rubi's sudden unemployment meant he had to change his lifestyle. He'd blown through all the money and gifts he'd received from his wives; his only remaining asset: the house on the left bank, which he sold to the banker Edmond de Rothschild for $400,000.

Ramfis even tried to meet Rubi in Paris but Rubi refused. In an interview, Rubirosa said that Ramfis had acted in a cowardly fashion by deserting his country at a critical time and that to him, Ramfis was dead. Of course, his anger was also motivated by the fraud incident in which Rubi lost half a million dollars.

[*Note*: That month in 1963, President John F. Kennedy was assassinated in Dallas.]

It is difficult to fathom how the President could not have known of the mob's plans for the Dominican Republic, but Bobby Kennedy was soon dogging Giancana. It is speculated in many media accounts, including movies and countless "conspiracy theories," that John Kennedy was assassinated partly because his brother was bearing down on the mob so hard.

Other theories postulate that the assassination was conducted by a combination of joint efforts including: the mob, the CIA, and other Federal security agencies.

Here are the key players: John F. Kennedy, Sam Giancana (the mob), Porfirio Rubirosa, the CIA, and the Dominican Republic and Castro. All of the events leading up to the Kennedy assassination and the players are tied together in one or more ways. Everyone, including Rubi, had his own agenda. Was Rubi involved in the assassination of his ex-father-in-law? Certainly, we know he had ties to those who wanted him dead and to the mob through Sinatra. He also had reasons to help or hinder Kennedy, depending upon which story you believe.

There is no one left to play with

9 Life Goes On Without Me

No matter how high or how fast he flies or how silky smooth the trip is, inevitably the gigolo must land back on earth. It is often a turbulent return to reality. Like Rubirosa, many of the dream kids who flew over the rainbow checked into that Mansion in the Sky as soon as their high-winding pace began to grind to a halt.

—Lynn Ramsey, *Gigolos*

In early 1964, Rubi and Odile moved to M a r n e s - l a - Cocquette, a small village outside of Paris. Their new abode was a humble and stark contrast to the mansion. There were no guest quarters, no servants, and no antiques (all of Doris' belongings had already been sold). It was simply furnished.

After a few months, friends began to report that Rubi had lost all his vitality and seemed extremely depressed, which is probably why he never finished his memoirs.

He continued to drink heavily as always, only now he would sleep for days. One day, at four in the afternoon, he began calling several of his friends to see if they wanted to play bocce. None of them could and he would remark to Odile that all his friends had seemed to instantly become factory workers. "There is no one left to play with."

Rubi was beginning to deteriorate without money, without the attention of women or his friends, and he would certainly never consider getting a job. According to Odile, "To work would have been a nightmare for Rubi."

Other friends argued that Rubi was on the comeback trail. They said he had plans to marry Patricia Kennedy Lawford, who had separated from Peter, or even Peggy Hitchcock, a Mellon heiress. For Rubi, life without money was sheer torture.

Oleg Cassini estimated that in Rubi's glory days, in the 1950s, the house, the servants and parties, the polo ponies, and the "gadabouting" from Saint Tropez to Deauville and Palm Beach, must have easily cost him $2 million a year.

Later that year, Rubi suffered another indignation when an invitation from a hotel in Florida to become the resort's public relations man, severely depressed him. Oddly enough, it was his old nemesis, Benitez Rexach, who had beaten him out of the old dredging contract that setup the appointment for Rubi.

Another venture, the launch of a line of fragrances called *Rubi*, to be sold in ruby-colored bottles, failed.

Still, life wasn't without its small adventures. In June 1965, Rubi and Odile were on Stavros Niarchos' three-masted schooner, the *Creole*, and the guests decided to create their own version of the James Bond movie, *Goldfinger.*

Rubi was chosen as the obvious lead, James Bond; Niarchos was Goldfinger; and Odile played Pussy Galore. They chartered a plane to shoot at the boat using 3,000 tennis balls in place of bullets but the balls were blown off course.

Gunther Sachs was the cameraman and he filmed the proceedings from a small boat, which promptly capsized and sank. Niarchos was too busy on the Teletype and he failed to deliver his lines while Rubi got too drunk to even stand.

Rubi now considered himself a pauper. In 1965, he complained about having only a meager income of $5,000 a month. That would be considered a fair amount for most people, but it was a pittance for Rubi.

Three weeks later, Rubi's polo team won a major tournament in France and to celebrate, he invited all his friends to

Le Calvados, a spot dear to his heart. Friends reported that it seemed more of a duty for Rubi, who appeared lethargic and even depressed.

Rubi had always been a heavy drinker, but he hadn't been stupid. Throughout his heydays, when he was drinking, he would always have a driver take him home. However, this particular evening was an exception.

As usual, Rubi was the last one to leave. Odile had gone home after midnight and most of the others were drifting out. He wasn't just alone in the room: He was solitary, inaccessible, his thoughts drifting off to what might have been.

Latin lover, man of intrigue, alleged spy, and toast of the café crowd—the greatest playboy of his age cries out in his loneliness to a world that has already forgotten him—a world that only cares, superficially.

It was eight a.m. when Rubi left the nightclub. We can almost hear the roar of his powerful engine as the exhaust bellows out the rasp of each gear winding out to maximum RPMs. Though he is relatively young, for Porfirio Rubirosa, time is running out. He has climbed drunkenly into his beloved silver Ferrari in the predawn hours, another night of debauchery behind him.

The Paris drizzle has made the streets as slick as an oiled runway and Porfirio's car begins to drift and slide from one lane to the other.

The crumpled Ferrari The jet-set life was catching up to him

Lost in his pain and anesthetized by alcohol, he begins to lose control of the car. With reflexes fully dulled, he loses consciousness as the Ferrari, now traveling at over 100 mph, jumps the curb on the Bois de Boulogne and slams into a chestnut tree.

The solid mahogany steering wheel crushes his chest. The scene is silent, save for the patter of rain on the roof of the car. A gray plume of smoke spews out from under the hood, and Porfirio lies paralyzed.

Within minutes, an ambulance arrives and is soon speeding to the hospital; Porfirio will not make it. He dies within sight of his two favorite recreation spots, the Bagatelle Polo Club and the Longchamps Race Course.

It was July 5, 1965. Rubi was 56.

Odile Rubirosa, right, during burial services
at Marnes la Coquette, near Paris.

Epilogue

To this day, some ask, "Was it suicide, murder, or simply the fast end to a fast life?"

Though he was Catholic, the Church declined to officiae over his funeral, citing his scandalous history. On July 8, 1965, Rubi was buried in a cemetery just a few meters from his home in Paris. His nephew, stone-faced, escorted Odile as she shed tears for her husband. Standing next to her in the pouring rain were JFK's sisters, Jean and Pat, who had come from New York for the funeral.

Princes, movie stars, politicians, playboys, and celebrities from all over the world gathered around the grave to pay their respects.

So brief and paradoxical was Rubi's life. He was colorful, yet miserable; wealthy *and* poor; surrounded by friends and yet so lonely. He enjoyed much as he sucked the marrow from the bones of life. Oddly, all his life he was chased by women and men alike, by kings and nobility—but in the end, he was denied a proper funeral.

On the surface, he always smiled and tried to please everyone. He had all the lovers and earthly delights he could ever ask for, yet ultimately, he was empty of spirit. Though he delighted in all the physical pleasures, he rarely nourished his soul.

It now seems odd to me that everyone was so surprised at how "minimalist" his funeral was, given the "church's" refusal to officiate. Men like Rubirosa don't need "proper" burials; it would go against the way they lived their lives: in Rubi's hedonistic case, first for love—second for attention— and third for money.

Odile returned to Hyannis Port with the Kennedy sisters. She was later remarried and lived in rural New England for quite some time. It was also reported that on his deathbed in 1969, Joseph Kennedy (JFK's father) summoned only two people to speak with—one was Odile. Perhaps we'll never know what was discussed, but from that point on Odile seemed to disappear into a quiet, private life. One rumor said she moved to Brazil. Other reports say she remarried and lives in the Maine area.

Hollywood is still chasing Rubi

R ubi's legacy lives in many ways in many locales; but to this day, perhaps the most fitting is when diners ask the waiter for a giant peppermill, more often than not, they ask for a Rubirosa, sometimes not even knowing the history behind that moniker.

We have investigated this man's life in this book and still others commemorate his existence in many ways. It is rumored that the actor Antonio Banderas is planning on producing and staring in a feature motion picture about Rubi and that there are several other books in the works.

In addition, there is a play, several discos, several cafes (most notably in Italy), an Italian racecar—and even several Web pages—named after him. In addition, people are still quoting him.

"Everything Rubirosa said had a fascinating and humorous sense. Once he said to a friend: 'If you want to meet a girl in the street, you tell her: Can you tell me where the across the street sidewalk is? She's going to find it weird and funny. A conversation can come and turn into a friendship or even a romance.'"

—Diogenes Reyna, Writer

On another occasion, writer Reyna said this as well:

"Dr. Rodriguez Brache, Dominican MD and personal friend of Rubirosa, said they used to play polo and spend much time together. He told me that 15 years after Rubirosa's death (1980), he went to Paris and made a reservation in the restaurant that they used to frequent together. The maitre'd said that the next opening wasn't for four months, so Brache said, 'I'm Dr. Rodriguez Brache, Rubirosa's friend who always came with me.'

"They not only gave him an immediate seat, it was a very special spot."

Perhaps the most poignant legacy, however, is Rubi's tombstone on which Odile had inscribed part of Psalm 144 from the Bible:

"Man is like a vanity. His days are like a shadow that passeth away."

✗

For Isabella and me, chasing Rubi was a 15-year labor of love. He still remains somewhat of an enigma, and we think that is the way that he wanted it. However, we did discover his secrets to lovemaking; the fact that he had a passion for polo and was an accomplished player; that he was a race-car driver, a diplomat, a pilot; played the violin, piano, guitar, and ukulele; was an adventurer, having gone on two daring sunken treasure hunts in exotic locals; and even had a talent for hypnosis and a bit of ESP.

Throughout his life of play, he was injured several times. He broke his neck in a polo fall, crash-landed both of his B-25 Bombers, broke his back in a racecar accident, and was shot twice just after World War II.

In all, he suffered at least five life-threatening injuries that we know of, and lived to play another day—and there's no way of telling how many narrow escapes he must have engineered from angry husbands.

We also know he was married five times, though perhaps, only twice for love. He also romanced many of the most beautiful celebrities in Hollywood and slept with hundreds of women.

In addition, we know that during his lifetime, he never truly worked at a real job, nevertheless, he did amass and spend more than $100 million (an astounding figure in today's dollars), a stable of expensive racing cars, polo ponies, and two converted B-25 Bombers. In the end, he died poor.

There are also many things we still don't know for sure. Did he smuggle Jews out of Germany during the war simply for profit, or were his motives more altruistic?

What really was his relationship with Trujillo? It appears throughout most of our investigations that each man derived what he needed from the other—a sort of symbiotic, unspoken, love-hate détente.

In an interview with the journalist Igor Cassini after Trujillo's assassination, Rubi was asked, "How did Dominicans feel about the Generalissimo's death?"

Rubi replied, "All you had to do was watch television to see the spontaneous outburst of grief registered by the people. I was in the streets and even as a Dominican I can tell you I was overwhelmed at the feelings of sorrow demonstrated by the people."

Cassini continued, "How were you personally affected by his death?"

"I was shocked, stunned. I had a great deal of affection and respect for him."

For some odd reason, even though Trujillo was gone, Rubi still, at least for a short period, felt compelled to continue to play the role of a supporter, even though most Dominicans certainly did not weep in the streets.

More questions: Was Rubi involved in the murders of two Dominican exiles? What really happened to Johnny Kohane during the liberation of the jewels in Spain? Did Rubi use his various diplomatic posts as fronts for a career of spying? What was his involvement in the Bay of Pigs situation? What did he know about the Kennedy assassination?

One of the most important questions that remains with me personally is: How does a man our own government accused of espionage with ties to murder and corruption, and gunrunners, end up on the President of The United State's private yacht partying with JFK and the Rat Pack?

The mystery continues, and we doubt the truth will ever be discovered. I remember the first day we began our research. Isabella spent the entire day at the New York Public Library in June of 1988. One of the prizes from that day's investigation was the discovery of the full page *New York Times* obituary filled with the jewels of Rubi's fast and amazing life.

I remember reading a single line on that page, which was what really peaked my curiosity.

"In almost a lifetime of pleasure seeking, Porfirio Rubirosa used a diplomatic portfolio, together with his appeal as a suave Latin romantic, as a passport to the high life on two continents."

If nothing else, this was a man who learned and mastered the art of using everything at his disposal for one purpose—pleasure.

During the years we conducted all our research, we endeavored to contact many of the people who knew Rubi best and are still often in the media, which just added to the long list of unanswered questions about Rubi.

Before we put this manuscript to bed, we contacted several of them, including Zsa Zsa, George Hamilton, Merv Griffin, Angie Dickenson, Ted Kennedy, and others.

George Hamilton once boasted in the press about Rubi being his mentor and idol, yet multiple conversations with his publicist and faxes to his home did not result in an interview. Makes you wonder what he might be hiding.

As for Danielle Darrieux, who currently resides in France, our correspondence with her yielded a very curt, "No, thank you. I do not wish to discuss my ex-husband."

None of those contacted wished to comment on Rubi, which was puzzling, and I am positive that whatever Joe Kennedy said to Odile Rodin on his deathbed, which has sealed her lips, will also forever remain a secret.

This may be the end of this book, but it isn't the end of this story. We have set up a Web site at www.chasingrubi.com to provide the more interested of you with the opportunity to follow our journey as we continue to try to answer questions about this man and his amazing life. And, for the true investigative reader, you can now download the complete Rubirosa FBI file and hundreds of documents and photographs that we have collected over the years.

There are many new FBI confidential papers included that have not been added to this book. These were just recently obtained. They contain, among other enlightening information, references to an INS investigation and the Bureau of Narcotics tying Rubi to possible drug and gunrunning activities.

There are also references, not included herein specifically, questioning the odd coincidence that not only did Rubi die as the result of a car crash, so did several of his friends including Prince Aly Khan and Amelio Tagle.

In closing, here is what happened to all the players in this story in later years:

Flor de Oro went on to marry eight more times after divorcing Rubi, and was later disinherited by her father and lived in exile for many years in Canada.

Ramfis Trujillo contracted pneumonia on Christmas Eve of 1969 and died on December 28. Just 10 days before, however, eight miles from Madrid, his car crashed head-on into an American's Jaguar. The owner, a woman, died instantly, but her two sons survived. Ramfis' face was smashed against the steering wheel. It is rumored that either the CIA or

President Joaquin Balaguer might have been behind the accident. Ramfis was buried in Madrid.

Danielle Darrieux.   In the '50s and '60s, she found several important roles, in films such as , *La Ronde* (1950), *Madame de* (1953) in which she gave her best performance; as a society lady torn between her husband and her lover; and *Demoiselles de Rochefort, Les* (1967). In 1970, she replaced Katharine Hepburn on Broadway in "Coco." Afterwards, she made occasional screen and stage appearances. However, she made a triumphant comeback in 2002, playing Catherine Deneuve's mother in the international hit *8 femmes* (2002).

She is still living in France.

Doris Duke.   After suffering from heart problems, Doris Duke died in her bed at Falcon Lair (her estate) in October of 1993 at the age of 80. She was later buried at sea. Following the funeral of this enigmatic woman, whiffs of "the butler did it" began to surface.

If nothing else, Doris Duke was considered a shrewd money manager and investor. She smartly parlayed her $30 million inheritance into a massive $750 million fortune. When she died, her entire estate was worth over one billion dollars.

Loving animals as she did, Doris ensured that they were provided for and that a $100,000 trust was set aside for her beloved dog. The majority of the money was earmarked for charity through the Doris Duke Charitable Foundation that supported the arts and environmental causes.

Barbara Hutton spent her life battling alcoholism, drug dependency, and anorexia, and her numerous, expensive divorces left her almost bankrupt. When the recluse finally died at age 66, she weighed less than 100 pounds and had only $3,000 of her fortune remaining.

Zsa Zsa Gabor still lives in Los Angeles. A friend of Zsa Zsa's recently visited her in her home and though she did not want to speak of the former love of her life, she did show off a beautifully framed photograph of Rubirosa mysteriously hanging in her dressing room behind a rack of evening gowns.

Inside the living-room-sized dressing room, Zsa Zsa pushed aside the gowns, looked at the Rubirosa photograph, smiled, winked with affection, and never spoke a word.

Odile Rodin lived in the New England area for a few years after Rubi's death. Not much is known about her after that with the notable exception of her being summoned to Joe Kennedy's deathbed and then her rumored move to Brazil. A source at *Vanity Fair* claims that in 2002 Odile remarried and is now living in Maine.

The Authors

Marty and Isabella Wall are a husband and wife writing team. They first became aware of, and intrigued by, the story of Porfirio Rubirosa more than 15 years ago because of stories told to Isabella by her father.

Isabella was born in the Dominican Republic and her father had lived in the same town as Rubi for many years. Her brother-in-law, who later became a political journalist in that country, also provided stories that continued to peak Isabella's interest in the man who would later become an international diplomat/playboy/spy for his country.

Both of these individuals have labored for years gathering research on Rubi, most notably by obtaining revealing heretofore-classified documents from the FBI through the Freedom of Information Act.

These documents helped to connect the many dots that had to that point, been an incomplete mosaic of information from others who knew, were married to, befriended, or romanced by Porfirio.

Marty Wall

Mr. Wall is the principle of M. Wall & Associates, a creative services company that serves the entertainment industry through the development and production of marketing campaigns. He has more than 25 years of experiencing in network and cable television.

Prior to the formation of M..Wall & Associates, Mr. Wall was senior vice president with the entertainment company, Pittard Sullivan, and was responsible for the overall creative and production direction of that company's worldwide client base including ABC and CBS Television.

The Primetime Emmy Awards recognized him in 1998 for his contributions to "The Wonderful World of Disney" for outstanding design.

In addition, Mr. Wall's writing experience included work on ABCs promotional campaigns for the TV series "Home Improvement," "The Drew Carey Show", and "Turner Classic Movies", among other well-known television projects.

During a 13-year promotion and marketing career in the radio and music industry, he was honored with the prestigious *Billboard Magazine*, Promotion Man of the Year for three years in the early 1990s.

Isabella Wall

Isabella Wall is the founder and president of Bella Quniceanera.com. She is a fashion model, actress and was the former Miss Dominican Republic. She recently appeared on "Days of Our Lives," "Nip/Tuck," and "ER."

She has also represented the Dominican Republic (she has been a U.S. citizen since 1999) in numerous international beauty pageants and subsequently as an informal ambassador for her country.

Mrs. Wall is also a professional event planner, an accomplished public relations agent, founder of Someone Cares International, and was one of Revlon's Most Unforgettable Women in 1992.

When she wasn't working in one of these capacities, she has been busy researching and writing *Chasing Rubi*.

(Above) **The Rubirosa children:**
Cesar, Ana and Porfirio
(Right) **Rubirosa's mother,** Ana
Ariza (Below) **The Rubirosa/
Trujillo wedding** press announce-
ment

Listín Diario
(Fundado el 1° de Agosto de 1889)

SANTO DOMINGO, R. D., MARTES, DICIEMBRE 8 DE 1952

Un Acto Social Esplendoroso constituyeron las Bodas de los jóvenes Rubirosa-Trujillo.

DISTINGUIDAS PERSONALIDADES DEL PAIS ASISTIERON A LA LUCIDA CEREMONIA NUPCIAL

EL JEFE DEL ESTADO Y LA
PRIMERA DAMA DE LA REPU-
BLICA, Y EL MINISTRO AMERI-
CANO Y SU DISTINGUIDA CON-
SORTE-APADRINARON-EL SUN-
TUOSO CASAMIENTO.

5011 A
ASSOCIATED PRESS PHOTO   FROM NEW YORK
CAUTION: USE CREDIT

DORIS DUKE, FIANCE AND HIS SISTER   9/47

AMERICAN TOBACCO HEIRESS DORIS DUKE (LEFT),
HER FIANCE, PORFIRIO RUBIROSA (CENTER), AND
HIS SISTER, ANITA, TALK IN THE DOMINICAN
LEGATION AT PARIS, FRANCE, SEPT. 1 , BEFORE
THE DUKE-RUBIROSA WEDDING. THE BRIDEGROOM IS
HONORARY CHARGE D'AFFAIRS AT THE DOMINICAN
LEGATION IN PARIS. THE BRIDE WORE A GREEN
.NGEABLE TAFFETA DRESS AND A GREEN VELVET

NEW DOMINICAN AMBASSADOR TO
ARGENTINA - B 3709 (NY27)

CELEBRATING THEIR/MOVE FROM FRANCE,
DORIS DUKE, (THE NEW MRS. RUBIROSA) AND
AMBASSADOR RUBIROSA DANCE AT A
PARTY THROWN IN THEIR HONOR.

note: event date/location to follow
                          — see DR
                          embassy

Doris and Rubi doing what rich people do.

FAMILY: W/wife

Mr. and Mrs. Porforio Rubirosa (Babs Hutton) arriving at the exclusive Club du Moulin Rouge in the
Palm Beaches. This is their first appearance in a
night spot since their marriage. Mrs. Rubirosa is
wearing an indian sari evening gown of biege and red
with gold embroidey, and she wore gold slippers.

1954

HORSE PLAY OR TRUE LOVE?

ZSA ZSA GABOR STANDS BY HER MAN,
PORFIRIORUBIROSA. THE COUPLE ARGUED
AT JIMMY'S NIGHTCLUB IN PARIS
LAST EVENING. RUBI ASKED HER TO
"LEAVE THE CLUB", WHICH SHE DID.
HOWEVER, THE CARRIBEAN CASANOVA AND
HUNGARIAN TEMPTRESS ARE BACK TOGETHER.
NEITHER ZSA ZSA'S HUSBAND, ACTOR GEORGE SANDERS,
OR MRS. RUBIROSA (BARBARA HUTTON) WERE AVAILABLE
FOR COMMENT.

OUTSIDE PARIS LOCATION: RUBIROSA'S MANSION

USE CREDIT

CAPTAIN OF THE DOMINICAN REPUBLIC'S TEAM

PLAYBOY-DIPLOMAT-POLO CHAMPION PORFIRIO RUBIROSA
IS A TOUGH GUY ON AND OFF THE POLO FIELD.
"RUBI" IS A TWO GOAL HANDICAPER WITH AN AGGRESSIVE
STYLE. OFF THE FIELD HE'S EQUALLY AGGRESSIVE ACCORDING
TO ZSA ZSA GABOR AND THE
FEDERAL BURUEA OF INVESTIGATION.

(PT/Dom Rep-7-1208)

PHOTO FROM DOMINICAN REPUBLIC 6-12-54 crg

NY 6/13/54

2N 7/5X

#3?

GABOR AND RUBIROSA IN CANNES

HOLLYWOOD'S ZSA ZSA GABOR IS SHOWN HERE
WITH PORFIRIO RUBIROSA, HUSBAND OF
BARBARA HUTTON, AFTER HE FLEW TO CANNES
TO JOIN HER AT THE FILM FESTIVAL THERE.
    THEY'RE SHOWN STROLLING THROUGH
THE SUNNY RIVIERA CITY A FEW DAYS AGO.

AP/PAR D7070   20454ERG   UKFOR
ASSOCIATED PRESS PHOTO FROM LONDON

N711-

sud 4/21
9067G

A 2840
ASSOCIATED PRESS PHOTO
CAUTION: USE CREDIT   FROM NEW YORK

RUBIROSAS AT DINNER

WHILE PORFIRIO/RUBIROSA AND HIS WIFE, ODILE,
DINED WITH MRS. NICOLAS ARROYO, LEFT, WIFE OF
CUBAN AMBASSADOR TO THE UNITED STATES AT A BEN
FIT LATE NOV. 21 IN NEW YORK, THIEVES MADE OFF
WITH JEWELRY WORTH $30,000 AND A MINK COAT FRO
THE RUBIROSA SUITE IN A MID-MANHATTAN HOTEL.
REPORT OF THE THEFT WAS MADE BY RUBIROSA AFTER
THE COUPLE RETURNED TO THEIR SUITE. INCLUDED
IN THE JEWELRY WAS A NECKLACE REPUTED TO BE
WORTH $23,000, ACCORDING TO POLICE. RUBIROSA
IS DOMINICAN REPUBLIC AMBASSADOR TO CUBA.

WIREPHOTOED N Y// 11-22-57

R/F   9A   11/22/58   STF-HVN   62

WTS NYWS14 MON ASB   LON ROM PAR ^ER S&S
SAMER20 MEX PR TMC NWK WW

with wife /57

PORFIRIO RUBIROSA, INTERNATIONAL
SOCIALITE AND SPORTSMAN, HAS BEEN APPOINTED
EXECUTIVE DIRECTOR OF MIAMI BEACH'S 600
ROOM DEAUVILLE HOTEL BY MORRIS LANSBURGH
OPERATOR OF THE SWANK NEW RESORT. DEAUVILLE
BEING BUILT BY SAM COHEN, AND WILL BE
COMPLETED DEC. 20, 1957. RUBIROSA IS SHOWN
WITH HIS BRIDE, THE FORMER ODILE RODIN,
BEAUTIFUL FRENCH MODEL.

6/57

B3809
ASSOCIATED PRESS ~~~~~~~~   FROM PARIS
CAUTION:USE CREDIT

RUBIROSA'S WIDOW LEAVES HOSPITAL

MRS. PORFIRIO RUBIROSA, CENTER, LEAVES A
PARIS HOSPITAL JULY 5 AFTER ANNOUNCEMENT
THAT HER HUSBAND, FORMER DOMINICAN DIPLOMAT
AND INTERNATIONAL PLAYBOY, HAD DIED FROM
INJURIES RECEIVED IN AN AUTO ACCIDENT.
RUBIROSA WAS FATALLY INJURED WHEN HIS CAR
STRUCK ANOTHER AND CAREENED INTO A TREE IN
THE BOIS DE BOULOGNE AREA IN THE WESTERN
EDGE OF THE FRENCH CAPITAL. WITH MRS. RUBIR
ARE A FRIEND,MRS. LACERDA (FIRST NAME
UNAVAILABLE) AND MRS. LACERDA'S CHAUFFEUR.
MRS. RUBIROSA,THE FORMER ODILE RODIN,WAS HI

FIFTH WIFE.
PR 7/5/65   918A   PW (52)

WT&S NYT NYW'S NR HD TYO STAATS SOU AMER ME
PR ZZ BAIRES TMC NWSWK WW

Photo Credits

Page xii.	CORBIS
Page xx.	LETRA GRAFICA
Page 29.	CORBIS
Page 60.	20th CENTURY FOX/PHOTOFEST
Page 87.	ASSOCIATED PRESS
Page 94.	ASSOCIATED PRESS
Page 100.	CORBIS
Page 103.	CORBIS
Page 111.	THURSTON HOPKINS/HULTON ARCHIVES/GETTY IMAGES
Page 112.	ASSOCIATED PRESS
Page 113.	PHOTOFEST
Page 120.	PARAMOUNT PICTURE/PHOTOFEST
Page 123.	PHOTOFEST
Page 139.	PHOTOFEST
Page 141.	GLOBE PHOTOS
Page 144.	CORBIS
Page 148.	2OTH CENTURY FOX/PHOTOFEST
Page 151.	HULTON ARCHIVES/GETTY IMAGES
Page 153.	CORBIS
Page 155.	PHOTOFEST
Page 162.	FPG/HULTON ARCHIVES/GETTY IMAGES
Page 167.	FPG/HULTON ARCHIVES/GETTY IMAGES
Page 170.	CORBIS
Page 172.	HULTON ARCHIVE/GETTY IMAGES
Page 174.	PHOTOFEST
Page 183.	CORBIS
Page 185.	SPRINGER/PHOTOFEST
Page 194.	PHOTOFEST
Page 196.	ASSOCIATED PRESS
Page 199.	KEYSTONE/HULTON ARCHIVES/GETTY IMAGES
Page 202.	FPG/HULTON ARCHIVES/GETTY IMAGES
Page 206.	PHOTOFEST

GALLERY PAGES CREDITS

Page 219	PHOTOFEST
	CORBIS
	PHOTOFEST
Page 220	ASSOCIATED PRESS
Page 221	LETRA GRAFICA
Page 222	MORGAN COLLECTION/HULTON ARCHIVES/GETTY IMAGES
Page 223	LETRA GRAFICA
Page 224	LETRA GRAFICA
Page 225	LETRA GRAFICA
Page 226	ASSOCIATED PRESS
Page 227	ASSOCIATED PRESS
Page 228	LETRA GRAFICA
Page 229	ASSOCIATED PRESS